Concise Encyclopedia of Church and Religious Organization Marketing

T0303953

Concise Encyclopedia of Church and Religious Organization Marketing

Robert Stevens
David Loudon
Bruce Wrenn
Henry Cole

Routledge
Taylor & Francis Group
New York London

First published by

Best Business Books® and The Haworth Reference Press™, imprints of The Haworth Press, Inc., 10 Alice Street, Binghamton, NY 13904-1580.

This edition published 2012 by Routledge

Routledge   Routledge
Taylor & Francis Group   Taylor & Francis Group
711 Third Avenue   2 Park Square, Milton Park
New York, NY 10017   Abingdon, Oxon OX14 4RN

PUBLISHER'S NOTE
The development, preparation, and publication of this work has been undertaken with great care. However, the Publisher, employees, editors, and agents of The Haworth Press are not responsible for any errors contained herein or for consequences that may ensue from use of materials or information contained in this work. The Haworth Press is committed to the dissemination of ideas and information according to the highest standards of intellectual freedom and the free exchange of ideas. Statements made and opinions expressed in this publication do not necessarily reflect the views of the Publisher, Directors, management, or staff of The Haworth Press, Inc., or an endorsement by them.

Cover design by Kerry E. Mack.

Library of Congress Cataloging-in-Publication Data

Concise encyclopedia of church and religious organization marketing / Robert E. Stevens . . . [et al.].
    p. cm.
    Includes bibliographical references and index.
    ISBN-13: 978-0-7890-1877-9 (hc. : alk. paper)
    ISBN-10: 0-7890-1877-2 (hc. : alk. paper)
    ISBN-13: 978-0-7890-1878-6 (pbk. : alk. paper)
    ISBN-10: 0-7890-1878-0 (pbk. : alk. paper)
    1. Church marketing—Encyclopedias. 2. Religious institutions—Marketing—Encyclopedias.
I. Stevens, Robert E., 1942-

BV652.23.C65 2005
206'.5—dc22

                                                                        2005011427

CONTENTS

            Bruce Wrenn
            Phylis Mansfeld

ABOUT THE AUTHORS

Robert Stevens, PhD, is Professor of Marketing in the Department of Management and Marketing at the University of Louisiana at Monroe. During his distinguished career, Dr. Stevens has taught at the University of Arkansas, the University of Southern Mississippi, and Hong Kong Shue Yan College. His repertoire of courses has included marketing management, business research, statistics, marketing research, and strategic management. The author or co-author of 20 books and well over 100 articles, he has published his research findings in a number of business journals and in numerous professional conference proceedings. He was co-editor of the *Journal of Ministry Marketing & Management,* is now co-editor of *Services Marketing Quarterly,* and serves on the editorial boards of four other professional journals. Dr. Stevens has acted as a marketing consultant to local, regional, and national organizations and is the owner of two small businesses.

David Loudon, PhD, is Professor of Marketing in the School of Business at Sanford University. He has also taught at the University of Louisiana at Monroe, Louisiana State University, the University of Rhode Island, Hong Kong Shue Yan College, and the North American Executive program in Monterrey, Mexico. He has taught a variety of courses but focuses on marketing management and consumer behavior. Dr. Loudon is the co-author of twelve books and has conducted research in the United States, Europe, Asia, and Latin America on such topics as consumer behavior, international marketing, services marketing, and marketing management. He has written over 100 papers, articles, and business cases, and his research findings have been published in a number of journals and in the proceedings of numerous professional conferences. He is co-editor of *Best Business Books,* an imprint of The Haworth Press, Inc., co-editor of *Services Marketing Quarterly,* and the past co-editor of *Journal of Ministry Marketing & Management.*

Bruce Wrenn, PhD, is Professor of Marketing in the School of Business and Economics at Indiana University South Bend. The author of several books on marketing management, planning, research, and marketing for religious organizations, Dr. Wrenn has also written numerous articles on marketing strategy, research, and marketing techniques for nonprofit, for-profit, and healthcare organizations. He spent several years with a major pharmaceutical company performing market analysis and planning and has served as a consultant to a number of industries, religious denominations, and organizations in the food, high-tech, and health care industries.

Henry Cole, PhD, is Associate Professor of Marketing and Chair of the Marketing Department at the University of Louisiana at Monroe, and previously taught at Hong Kong Shue Yan College. He has taught a variety of marketing courses including marketing principles, industrial marketing, personal selling, advertising, retailing, and marketing management. The president of a small business, Dr. Cole has authored or co-authored several papers and articles in journals and the proceedings of professional conferences.

Preface

Marketing has come of age for many nonprofit organizations in recent years. This is evidenced by the large number of publications aimed at those organizations. Journals as well as books on marketing of health care, education, and professional services attest to the growing recognition of the application of marketing to many nontraditional and nonbusiness areas. However, one area in which only limited published application of marketing exists is for churches and religious organizations.

This book is intended to be a basic reference guide to those interested in church and religious marketing. The topics and discussion provide a brief introduction to basic terminology and concepts used in marketing churches and religious organizations.

Acknowledgments

A book is seldom the work of the authors alone, but reflects inputs from many sources. We would especially like to express our appreciation to the following people for their help in preparing drafts of the book: Rajni Nair, Avni Patel, and Alana Truelove.

ACCESS

Every church and religious organization must make decisions about how best to provide access to its services and programs. In marketing terms, this is often referred to as place or distribution decisions. Most organizations face the problem of where they should be located to best serve the diverse groups of constituents that are ministered to through their organization.

Other aspects of access involve the level of service and the number and location of branches or satellite facilities. Each organization must decide on the level of service it intends to provide to constituents. The level of service refers to the availability of the organization's services or programs to its constituents. For example, local church administrators must decide how many times a week to offer services to their congregation. Some members may prefer to have services only once a week, while others want services available daily. An organization that ministers to the poor and needy through preparing meals must decide the schedule of meals. Are they to be offered once, twice, or three times daily, or offered on a weekly basis?

Another area is personal contacts. Will personal contacts be made with every visitor? Most organizations try to qualify prospective members by having visitors fill out some type of visitor card to identify those they want to call on or to allow visitors to request a personal contact.

These decisions bring about significant personnel and cost implications. A higher level of service must be funded at a greater level, and requires more personnel to implement. On the other hand, lower levels of service can be offered with fewer personnel and smaller funding. The decision must involve a trade-off between what the organization wants to do and can do, given the funds and personnel available. Starting at a lower level and increasing to higher levels is a better plan. This permits learning how to improve service delivery, and also avoids taking away services from constituents due to funding/personnel shortages.

The organization must decide whether to centralize its services or offer services through many alternate facilities. The most economical decision is to operate a single facility. By having one large facility, duplication of services, staff, and building costs are avoided. Constituents benefit by a higher quality of service, but pay the price of having to travel longer distances.

The costs of operating an organization are usually minimized by a central facility. However, as population shifts and new programs are added, the pressure for satellite facilities increases. Some churches develop a mission church, which they staff until the congregation size is large enough to have its own ministerial staff.

Additional facilities must be carefully analyzed, because the added financial and staff needs can affect the organization's ability to maintain quality in many separate facilities. However, to effectively minister to diversely scattered groups, satellite facilities or some type of mobile unit must be utilized.

ACTIVE LISTENING

Active listening consists of a continuous, systematic collection of information from both providers and recipients of church ministries. The objective of conducting active listening processes is to keep decision makers constantly aware of the experiences of those involved in the delivery of ministry services, as well as the expectations and perceptions of individuals receiving those services. A fundamental premise of conducting active listening is that decision makers are both seriously interested in learning about those experiences and perceptions, as well as committed to making decisions based upon the findings of that inquiry. That is, it makes little sense to engage in active listening unless what is heard ultimately plays a role in influencing decisions and plans. Table 1 identifies the relevant methods that might be used in an active listening system.

TABLE 1. Research Approaches for Building an Active Listening System

Research approach	Description	Purpose	Limitations
New, inactive, and lost member surveys	Surveys to determine why church members chose the church, are inactive, or have left the church.	Assess the role various ministries play in attraction and building loyalty.	Church must be able to identify, locate, and get cooperation of respondents.
Focus group interviews	Moderated sessions of 8 to 12 people who are homogeneous along some variable of interest (e.g., gender, involvement in church activities, leaders, etc.).	Discussion topics focus on a specific topic. Provides fast feedback on activities undertaken, suggestions or ideas being considered.	Good for generating ideas, hypotheses, general barometer of opinions; not good for projecting to larger population of interest. Moderator must be skilled at conducting groups.
Advisory panels	A group of church members or people in the community who agree to provide feedback on selected church activities or ideas for future activities.	Obtain in-depth, timely feedback from interested parties.	Recruitment and maintenance of panel; panelists may not be representative of population of interest.
Complaint, comment, and inquiry capture	An information system to retain, categorize, track, and distribute communications to church decision makers from members, leaders, the community, etc.	Identify areas where delivery of ministries or other church services require attention or improvement.	Does not capture instances where dissatisfaction is not volunteered. Provides only a partial picture.
Leadership surveys	Surveys of church leaders to determine their impressions of ministry effectiveness.	Measure internal perception of ministry quality; obstacles to delivery of ministries; identify root causes of problems.	Leaders see quality through a biased perspective.

Source: Adapted from Berry, Leonard L., *Discovering the Soul of Service* (New York: The Free Press), 1999, pp. 100-102.

SUGGESTED READING

Berry, Leonard L. and A. Parasuraman, "Listening to the Customer—The Concept of Building a Service-Quality Information System," *Sloan Management Review,* Spring 1997, p. 66.

ADOPTION PROCESS

The adoption process is a group of stages through which a constituent passes before repeatedly attending a church. This is a step-by-step approach to a final decision.

1. *Awareness:* A constituent first learns of a church or ministry, often through advertising. However, other means can be used to gain awareness. For example, the movie, *The Passion of the Christ,* used publicity to make people aware of the movie.
2. *Interest:* The constituent gathers information and details about the church.
3. *Evaluation:* The constituent determines the costs and benefits of attending in relation to his or her personal needs.
4. *Trial:* The potential member experiences the church for the first time, by either attending or by watching the church service on television.
5. *Adoption:* After the trial is considered successful, the constituent makes a decision to attend/watch on a regular basis.
6. *Repeat:* The constituent continues to weigh expectations against experiences, but will repeat behavior if needs continue to be met.

Through the stages in the adoption process, potential churchgoers may "drop out" along the way. For example, even though many people are aware of a church, they may never visit (trial) because they do not think it will satisfy their needs. There will usually be "dropouts" at each stage. All constituents should be made to feel welcome and communicated with at all stages. Even those who are adopters and repeatedly attend need follow-up contacts.

The promotional message at each stage should encourage a continued relationship. A guide to creating these messages is AIDA. The acronym is a time-honored model for the steps in the promotional process. A message should:

> attract **A**ttention,
> hold **I**nterest,
> build a **D**esire,
> and produce **A**ction.

This approach to promotion planning coincides with the adoption process consumers go through in making decisions about religious organizations.

ADVERTISING MESSAGE

An advertising message is simply what is communicated (verbally and nonverbally) by an ad. This information is transmitted from the sender (advertiser) to the audience, and is both what is said and how it is said. The message is one of the elements of advertising strategy.

Before a message is created, an advertising strategy should be developed and put in a concise, written statement called the creative brief. This is a guide for creating and producing an ad. Advertising agencies sometimes refer to the creative brief as the copy (or creative) platform, work plan, creative contract, or creative blueprint. The creative brief is comprised of the advertising objective, the basic issue the advertising must address, the major idea or benefit, the target audience, and the supporting information and requirements.

The next step after the creative brief is the creative process, during which the message strategy is developed. The message strategy deals with what the ad communicates and how it is communicated; that is, the message is both words and art. The message should adhere to the advertising strategy stated in the creative brief.

Creativity is needed to produce an effective advertising message. To create means to cause to come into existence, to originate. Creativity can help advertising to break through mental perceptual screens, to inform, to persuade, and to remind.

An important part of creating the advertising message is to develop the major selling idea. This idea is the single most important thing that can be said about the product. If presented in a unique manner, it gets attention, produces a reaction, and sets the product apart from other products.

Message strategies can be cognitive or affective. A cognitive message strategy uses rational reasons such as tangible benefits for choosing the product. An affective message strategy creates emotions and feelings, which lead to or relate to the product. Various appeals can be used in the message to motivate or excite the target audience. Common appeals are love, fear, nostalgia, safety, health, comfort, sex, convenience, economy, patriotism, luxury, efficiency, and accomplishment.

The advertising messages can be presented in a number of ways called executional frameworks. Some examples include the following:

- *Testimonial:* A satisfied user tells about the effectiveness of the church or program
- *Credible presenter:* An expert or celebrity adds credibility by presenting the message
- *Informative:* Information is presented in a straightforward manner
- *Demonstration:* The product is shown in action
- *Fantasy:* A make-believe situation (e.g., animation) expresses the message
- *Slice-of-life:* The product provides solutions to everyday, real-life problems and situations
- *Dramatization:* This method uses an exaggerated situation, music, or lifestyle techniques to present the message

Generally the message of an ad should get the attention of the audience and build interest in the product. It should establish credibility and desire for the product. Finally, the audience should be motivated to action.

ATMOSPHERE

Atmosphere refers to the physical aspects of an organization's buildings and grounds. Such factors as color, lighting, noise, odors, layout of rooms, and seating have an effect on people's perceptions of an organization. Obviously, well-kept grounds and buildings present a better image than those that are poorly kept. But the impact of physical surroundings is much greater than that.

First, consider the impact of color. Every color sends out its own wavelengths when exposed to light. Each waveband stimulates chemicals in the eye, sending impulses to the pituitary and pineal glands near the brain. Stimulated by the response to a color, glandular activity may speed up or slow down heart rates, increase or decrease brain activity, and alter the moods of the recipient of the wavelengths. The impacts of various colors include the following:

- *Blue:* Decreases breathing and pulse rate; causes tranquility; too much and rather dark shades of blue may cause depression
- *Bright red:* Increases heartbeat; causes overstimulation; makes people irritable, bad-tempered, and anxious
- *Bright yellow:* Raises blood pressure, pulse, and respiration
- *Drab gray:* Slows heartbeat; causes lethargy and depression
- *Brown:* A relaxing color, associated with comfort
- *Dark shades:* Affect people's sense of time passage; make time seem to pass more slowly
- *Light shades:* Affect people's sense of time passage; make time seem to pass faster
- *Pink:* A temporary pacifier; after a short time period, it seems to foster aggressiveness

An issue dealt with by many organizations, especially churches and ministries, is audio levels. The acoustics and sound systems in a room present challenges to even professional audio companies. Complaints of music being too loud or not loud enough are common in most congregations. Sound levels are measured in decibels (dB). To avoid hearing damage, the noise level should be no more than 74 dB for an average eight-hour day. Damage to hearing begins at 75 dB.

The layout of buildings, especially large complexes, may create problems for members, newcomers, and visitors. Many churches have built additions or new buildings as growth has occurred. Unless carefully planned, these additions can make people feel disoriented or lost. The use of signs and greeters at strategic points to guide people through the complex is extremely important in these situations. Another issue is movement of people from one area to another. For example, if a church has two morning services, traffic jams can occur between those leaving the first service and those attending the second service. If a rear exit from the sanctuary is available, attendees can be trained to exit there to avoid traffic jams.

ATTITUDE MEASUREMENT

Church decision makers might want to determine the attitudes or opinions of members, recipients of ministries, prospective members, church leaders, people in the community, etc. In such instances, knowledge of the appropriate research methodology for attitude measurement is important.

Attitudes are one of the most frequently measured items of interest to marketing decision makers. Why the interest in attitudes? Because marketing decision makers believe that the way people think (i.e., their attitude), and what they are likely to do (i.e., their behavior) are closely related. Why, then, don't we just study behaviors, since we are ultimately interested in understanding and influencing a person's behavior, not just their attitudes? Several reasons why we focus on attitudes instead of exclusively on behavior are:

1. Marketers may not have access to observation or self-reports of a person's behavior. The behavior may occur over a long period of time or in private settings only, and therefore observation is either not possible or is prohibitively expensive. Also, sometimes the behavior itself is of a nature that people will not voluntarily report it, but will answer attitude questions related to the behavior.
2. Sometimes the behavior cannot be reported because it has not yet occurred. If, for example, church decision makers are considering significant changes in the worship service, they might prefer measuring member attitudes to the change instead of making the changes and measuring attendance as a gauge of the popularity of the change.
3. Attitudes can help us understand *why* certain behaviors are likely to occur. This diagnostic quality to attitudes can be very helpful when designing programs intended to influence the behaviors of a target audience.
4. Under certain circumstances, attitudes can be loosely related to behavior. Research has shown that the usage rate for a product

or service is associated with the favorableness of a person's attitude; when attitudes are unfavorable, a person is more likely to discontinue use of a product or service; and when attitudes are based on actual experience rather than exposure to an advertisement, attitudes have been shown to more accurately predict behavior. (McDaniel and Gates, 2002, p. 314)

Several factors determine just how well attitudes can predict behavior, including the following:

- Level of involvement of the person with the ministry program: Prediction increases with involvement level
- Quality of the measurement process: Measuring specific rather than abstract attitudes, measuring closely in time to the behavior, and using valid and reliable measuring devices all increase predictive ability
- Influence of other people on the person: How motivated the individual is to comply with norms versus act on their own attitudes toward something
- Interference of situational factors: Prediction decreases when situational factors such as illness intervene between attitudes and behavior
- Strength of the attitude: The more strongly held the attitude the more predictive it is of behavior (McDaniel and Gates, 2002, p. 315)

What to Measure

A primary consideration in the measurement of attitudes is whether to measure a person's attitude toward an *object* or toward a *behavior.* Under the attitude-toward-object model a person's attitude toward an "object"—a church, ministry, or program—is a function of how much he or she knows about the object of attention, what he or she feels are important characteristics of the object, and whether he or she believes a particular version of the object possesses those characteristics. So, for example, if you were measuring someone's attitude toward a church using the attitude-toward-object model, you might use an approach similar to the following:

Compared to other churches, Trinity Church is:

Friendly	Unfriendly
Conservative	Liberal
Pleasant	Unpleasant
Youthful	Old
Vibrant	Stuffy

The other model is the attitude-toward-behavior model. Here, the intent is to measure someone's attitude about actually performing a particular behavior. An example of this measurement would be:

Attending Trinity Church would be a *pleasant* experience	Very likely	Very unlikely
Attending Trinity Church would be a *friendly* experience	Very likely	Very unlikely

Another consideration of what to measure concerns the subcomponents of attitudes. Specifically, attitudes consist of three components—affective, cognitive, and conative—and any measures of attitudes should include questions that measure all three parts. The affective component involves feelings, the cognitive involves beliefs, and the conative involves a predisposition to behave in a particular way. An example:

	Strongly Agree	Agree	Neither	Disagree	Strongly Disagree
Affective: I enjoy the church's musical programs	___	___	___	___	___
Cognitive: I believe the sermons strengthen my faith	___	___	___	___	___
Conative: I want to be more involved in church activities	___	___	___	___	___

How to Measure

Attitude measurement is typically accomplished in a survey intended to measure other variables of interest such as behavior, intentions, awareness, knowledge, demographics, etc. By measuring multiple variables of interest in the same survey, cross-tabulation can be used to compare answers by different types of respondents. For example: Do young people hold different attitudes toward the music during church services than older people? Do people who attend regularly have different attitudes about church finances than sporadic attendees? etc. Attitudes are measured using one of several scales designed for their purpose. (*See also* SCALES for details.)

REFERENCE

McDaniel, Carl and Roger Gates, *Marketing Research,* Fifth Edition (Cincinnati: South-Western), 2002.

SUGGESTED READING

Ajzen, Icek and Mortin Fishbein, *Understanding Attitudes and Predicting Social Behavior* (Upper Saddle River, NJ: Prentice Hall), 1980.

BENEFITS OF MARKETING

The basic reason an organization should be interested in applying marketing principles is that they will enable it to achieve its objectives more effectively. Organizations in our country depend upon voluntary exchanges to accomplish their objectives. Marketing is the discipline concerned with managing exchanges effectively and efficiently.

Marketing produces several major benefits for the organization and its constituents.

1. Many organizations lack the tools needed to satisfy their constituents, and may deliver unsatisfactory services which people accept because there are no alternatives. In many instances, administrators simply do not know how to improve on what they are currently offering. Marketing, which focuses on the importance of measuring and satisfying constituent needs, tends to produce an improved level of service and satisfaction.
2. Organizations, in striving to satisfy a set of constituents, must attract various resources, including members, volunteers, employees, funds, and, sometimes, public support. Marketing provides an approach to improving the organization's ability to attract needed resources.
3. Marketing places a great emphasis on rational management and coordination of programs, contributions, communication, and access. Many organizations make these decisions with insufficient knowledge, resulting in either more cost for the given impact or less impact for the given cost. The scarcity of funds in most churches and ministries means that the maximum results must be achieved per dollar expenditure.
4. Marketing's focus on the coordination of activities and concentration on constituents' needs usually produces more efficient efforts from activities. If constituents receive the right communications, the amount can be reduced. Marketing aids in identifying what the right messages are and, therefore, improves efficiency.

BRAND EQUITY

A brand is a name, term, or method of identification that distinguishes a product, service, or organization from all others. Equity is the value of property above and beyond what is owed on it. Therefore, brand equity is the intangible value of a product or an organization above and beyond the physical net assets. The name of a church or ministry (its brand) has value just as a brand of product has value. Brand equity is the added value that a name gives a church. In effect, it is what people think and feel, in total, about the organization. "Goodwill" is synonymous with brand equity.

For a church, brand equity helps produce awareness, perceived quality, and loyalty. A church with a good name in the community will have more people considering it as a church home. Its membership will be more committed and less likely to leave. A church with a high level of brand equity will not suffer from as much member-switching behavior because other churches may not be viewed as being of equal quality.

To increase brand equity, a church must develop its strategy, communicate its uniqueness, and deliver on its promises. It must differentiate itself, promote itself, and perform in such a way as to positively touch people's lives. Often, brand equity is built on a characteristic or benefit that is superior to the competition. Investments of time, effort, and money are generally required, but the benefits of brand equity can be extremely valuable and result in a competitive advantage.

BUDGETS

Marketing efforts require expenditures of funds that need to be budgeted. In other words, an administrator should budget these expenditures to ensure that the financial support needed to undertake marketing activities is available. The three most commonly used methods are: the percentage of revenues or contributions approach, the "all you can afford" approach, and the task or objective approach.

One of the most common budgeting approaches for marketing is to use a percentage of revenue or contributions. The budget is determined by applying a fixed percentage to either past or forecasted income. The proportion of revenues allocated to marketing may be based upon past results or on administrative judgments about the future.

This method is widely used for many reasons. Besides being simple to calculate, it is exact and is easy to define by administrators who are used to thinking of costs in percentage terms. Also, it is financially safe, since it ties expenditures directly to contributions.

The major problem with the percentage approach is its inherent fallacy to view marketing as a *result* rather than a *cause* of contributions. But this method can legitimately be used as a starting point for budgeting and can offer good direction in this process.

Some organizations set marketing budgets on the basis of available funds. In this instance, the organization spends as much as it can afford without impairing financial stability. Thus, the budget adopted and the monies needed to accomplish the required marketing task may be totally unrelated. On the one hand, the organization could miss opportunities because of underspending, while on the other hand; it could easily spend too much.

None of the methods are without major fault, and none closely approximates a good standard. The task or objective approach—or the *build-up* approach, as it is often called—has the most merit. This method requires that marketing objectives be stated well, and then the expenditures necessary to reach these objectives be determined. The implementation of such a method is somewhat more complex, but the end result is that only what is needed in a given time period is spent. Using this approach, you spend only what is needed to accomplish the stated objectives. This approach requires a great deal of experience in terms of knowing what can be accomplished with a specific level of expenditures.

CAUSE-RELATED MARKETING

Is not this the fast that I choose:
    to loose the bonds of injustice,
    to undo the thongs of the yoke,
to let the oppressed go free,
    and to break every yoke?
Is it not to share your bread with the hungry,
    and bring the homeless poor into your house;
when you see the naked, to cover them,
    and not to hide yourself from your own kin?

Isaiah 58:6-7 NRSV

Religious organizations have long felt the call to be an integral part of achieving positive social change. Marketers saw the application of marketing theories to social causes much more recently. The first books with related titles appeared in the early 1970s. The first formal definition of social marketing was "the design, implementation, and control of programs calculated to influence the acceptability of social ideas and involving considerations of product planning, pricing, communication, distribution, and marketing research" (Kotler and Zaltman, 1971, p. 5).

Inevitably, marketing has become a tool used to promote social causes—given the common goal of both marketers and agents of social change—to effect a change in people's behavior. Neither party is satisfied with merely changing attitudes, they seek to get a targeted group of people to make a commitment to a different set of actions than they previously pursued. Although the use of marketing to further social causes has not been without controversy, it is now generally seen as another useful tool to more effectively achieve the adoption of the behavior fostered by the advocates of the social cause. Some examples of social causes, which have been effectively marketed, include

Family planning	Nature conservancy
Energy conservation	Safety belt usage
Carpooling	Abstinence
Fire prevention	Vegetarianism
Literacy	Child adoption
Obesity prevention	Alcoholism control
Physical fitness	Antismoking
Animal rights	

These examples illustrate that the behaviors that social cause marketers seek to influence do not benefit the marketer, but rather the target market itself as well as society as a whole. Moreover, marketers of social causes might seek to affect opposing behaviors in the same audience (e.g., pro-choice or pro-life abortion advocates). Our goal here is not to debate the choice of social causes to be marketed, or the appropriateness of marketing to be applied to social causes, but rather to identify what is unique about social cause marketing and resources useful to those seeking to learn more about its successful application.

Reasonable Goals

Perhaps the most important first thing to understand about the use of marketing of social causes is that marketing, even at its best, cannot work miracles. People who are highly resistant to a change in their behavior, either to stopping a behavior or starting a behavior, will be resistant to marketing appeals as well, no matter how artfully conceived. In general, marketers are more likely to have success in changing behaviors that are low-involvement, one-time, and individual decision (e.g., donating money to help fund a church youth group trip to Washington, DC), as opposed to those that are high-involvement, continuing, and group decisions (e.g., becoming a member of a marriage ministry team). Marketing plans, no matter how expertly developed, will inevitably have greater success with the former compared to the latter behaviors in persuading people not initially predisposed to changing their behaviors.

Suggestions for Social Cause Marketers

Some suggestions for marketers of social causes:

1. Do not fool yourself about something people "should" want, give them something they really do need.
2. Make their success in adopting the desired behavior easy—easy to understand, easy to find other people adopting the same behavior, easy to do, easy to see the positive results from adopting the behavior, etc.
3. Make success in adopting the desired behavior rewarding. Reinforce the behavior by providing rewards and support for its adoption.
4. Make the behavior part of the communal process—what normal, respectable people do.
5. Work on moving people through the stages of behavioral adoption. If they have moved past awareness, do not continue to stress that, work on getting interest or trial.
6. Maintain relationships with other interested parties. Make sure all parties invested in the behavioral change continue to be motivated and coordinated.

7. Use the proper mix of marketing tools. Do not stress promotion alone to the exclusion of the other components of the marketing mix.
8. Be prepared for the long haul. Sustained behavioral change requires a long-term commitment, and measures of success might demand an equivalent perspective.
9. Institutionalize the process. Make sure that when outside financial and intellectual support ends, the "small groups" are able to continue to market the social cause.
10. Build bridges and choose your battles carefully. You are not alone in wanting to effect positive social change. Find others to ally with in your quest and do not let trivial differences get in the way of your joint success. Fight only those battles that involve principles that are central to your perspective of the cause you are promoting. (Smith, 1989, p. 5)

REFERENCES

Kotler, Philip and Gerald Zaltman, "Social Marketing: An Approach to Planned Social Change," *Journal of Marketing,* 35 (July) 1971, pp. 3-12.
Smith, William, *Communication and Marketing for Child Survival* (Washington, DC: Academy for Educational Development), August 8, 1989, p. 5.

SUGGESTED READING

Andreasen, Alan R., *Marketing Social Change* (San Francisco, CA: Jossey-Bass), 1995.

COMMUNICATION METHODS

Communication methods refer to the way an organization communicates to its constituents. An organization can use two basic communication methods to promote its programs and services: nonpersonal contact and nonpersonal contact.

Nonpersonal contact includes advertising, signs, brochures, displays, and publicity. Because most organizations use more than one method, they develop a communications mix to provide a complete communications program. The relative emphasis on personal contact and nonpersonal contact is determined by the type of information to be delivered.

Personal contact permits a chance for an exchange of information—a give-and-take situation. The personal contact allows constituents to ask questions important to them. Although nonpersonal contact may be used to build constituent awareness and provide information on the organization and its services, the complete communications message may need to be delivered by an individual. This is especially true when there are complex questions or special needs of constituents. If an extremely large and diverse group of constituents exists, the importance of nonpersonal communications may increase, but personal contact is still important in many cases. For example, many national television evangelists have area representatives who provide personal contact and counseling.

For other ministries, the major emphasis is on nonpersonal contact because of large geographically dispersed groups of constituents. Even though the cost of an individual TV program may be $100,000, if 5 million constituents were reached by the message, the cost per contact would be very low compared to the cost of a personal contact with each constituent. Personal contact may also include telephone calls or responses to letters.

Thus, the mix of the various methods is determined by the nature of the service and the needs and location of the constituents. Although both methods are needed and used, one is usually emphasized more heavily in one organization than another.

COMPETITION

The subject of competition could well be the topic most likely to make many of the readers of this book uncomfortable. This could be because they prefer to think of all like organizations as contributing to achievement of goals common to religious organizations rather than as competitors. Such a perspective is understandable and perhaps even laudable, although it has been known to vanish when other organizations competing for the same resources do not play fair, or are seen as succeeding at the expense of one's own organization. Understanding the nature of competition allows religious organizations to make a more informed decision about whether, how, and when to react in a competitive situation.

Levels of Competition

A religious organization can face competition on at least four levels:

1. *Desire competitors*—other immediate desires that a person might want to satisfy. At this level all religious organizations are, in fact, fighting a common competitor for the hearts and minds of people. When people look for meaning to life outside of religion, seek answers to life's most profound questions without spiritual guidance, or pursue lifestyles devoid of redeeming social value, the competition has "won."
2. *Generic competition*—other basic ways in which a person can satisfy a desire. Here, different philosophies (e.g., new age, humanism) or different forms of religion compete.
3. *Form competitors*—other forms of satisfying the same particular desire. At this level the religious organization competes with similar organizations (e.g., Christian with Christian, Jewish with Jewish, etc.).
4. *Institution competitors*—other institutions offering the same form of satisfaction (e.g., other Methodist churches, other Christian adoption agencies, etc.).

Seen in this light, most religious organizations do desire to more effectively compete at least at some level or levels in order to achieve their basic mission. In fact, a case could be made that failure to compete successfully on at least the desire level is to be unfaithful to the founding purpose of most religious organizations. Competitive activity will take different forms at each competitive level.

Competition at the desire level.

This level is characterized by cooperation with other religious organizations to pool resources to demonstrate the value of religion as a source for meaning. Sometimes the objective is to get people to stop performing some destructive behaviors (e.g., drug abuse, prostitution, child abuse), other times it is to direct behavior to more positive behaviors (e.g., spending time in prayer, performing acts of kindness, etc.). (*See* CAUSE-RELATED MARKETING for some ideas of how to compete successfully at this level.)

Competition at the generic level.

This level is characterized by demonstrating that a particular form of religion (e.g., Christianity), is preferable over other philosophies or religions (e.g., new ageism). Here, too, cooperation with other organizations of the same religious type allows the use of pooled resources to foster a common goal. Successful competition at this level would involve demonstrations of how individuals could better achieve their goals through that religion than the competition (e.g., why Christianity is "better" than adopting a new age philosophy).

Competition at the form level.

This level is characterized by providing a compelling rationale for becoming a member of a particular religious-affiliated body (e.g., denomination or religious association). This is equivalent to corporate-level marketing conducted in the for-profit sector. Successfully competing at the form level requires demonstration that the organization can provide more benefits salient to the individual than other form-level competitors.

Competition at the institutional level.

This level is characterized by marketing a "competitive advantage" of that institution (e.g., a particular Baptist church in a specific town) over other similar institutions (e.g., other Baptist churches in the same town). (*See* COMPETITIVE ADVANTAGE for ideas on how to compete successfully at this level.)

Religious organizations often acknowledge the need to compete successfully in order to accomplish their missional goals, and will see the desirability of competing at more than one of the four levels, perhaps at all four levels simultaneously. Attempting such a competitive strategy requires the organization to marshall its resources carefully, collaborating whenever possible with other organizations facing the same competitors, and maintaining a clear objective for each level of competition. Setting such objectives means that the religious organization has obtained an understanding of the needs, motives, influences, and decision processes used by the target market members who are choosing among competitors at the competitive level in question. For example, a religious organization seeking to counsel people to choose a different way of dealing with stress than spouse abuse must fully understand why people react to stress in this way if they are to win this competitive battle. In contrast, if a particular church, in competition with another church across town wants to attract a young couple to its church, it must have a solid understanding of what factors will influence the couple's choice. At this "institutional level," competition is where the tools of marketing segmentation, targeting, positioning, and the use of the marketing mix of programs, promotion, location, and "pricing" will most prominently come into play. However, marketing thought can contribute to an organization's ability to successfully compete at any of the four levels.

SUGGESTED READING

Stevens, Robert and David Loudon, *Marketing for Churches and Ministries* (Binghamton, NY: The Haworth Press), 1992.

COMPETITIVE ADVANTAGE

The search for competitive advantage lies at the heart of all marketing strategy. In fact, if you have no sustainable competitive advantage you will not be able to succeed.

Thus, the question that is central to the search for a competitive advantage has relevance for organizations of all types: "Why should someone engage in exchange with us rather than another organization?" The answer must be "Because they value what we do more than they do our competitors." (*See* COMPETITION to learn of the various levels upon which religious organizations can conceptualize competition.) Having a competitive advantage, therefore, hinges on providing something that is seen as having greater value in the eyes of your target audience than anything else they could obtain from another source to address the need they are seeking to have satisfied. This thinking may be alien to most leaders of religious organizations, but most will recognize that the answer to the central question of "Why should someone engage in exchange with us rather than any other organization?" must be something other than "Because we really, really want them to." Thus, at some level the concept of searching for and establishing a reason to justify why limited resources (time, allegiance, money, effort, etc.) should be provided to your organization could be a fruitful exercise.

Several conditions have been established for determining if you have a "real" competitive advantage (Cohen, 1995, p. 36):

1. The advantage(s) must be real. Just wishing it to be there does not make it true. This means you must be objective and dispassionate when looking at what your organization's special competencies are when compared to other organizations competing for the same resources. Perhaps getting someone who is outside your organization to appraise your organization's ability to perform the competency in question would be helpful in determining how "real" is the advantage.

2. The advantage(s) must be important to the person (or organization) that you wish to engage in exchange. (*See* EXCHANGE for more on the nature of exchange processes for religious organizations.) In for-profit enterprises, competitive advantages exist only when they ultimately translate into a benefit that the customer seeks and values. Merely being different from competitors along some dimension that you, the organizational decision makers, think is important does not mean that you have a true competitive advantage. The implication here is that you must have a means of understanding how your target audience thinks, feels, attaches VALUE and makes choices. Obtaining that understanding requires knowledge of CONSTITUENT BEHAVIOR and research methods. (*See* ATTITUDE MEASUREMENT, FOCUS GROUPS, PRIMARY DATA, QUESTIONNAIRE, and SCALES.)

3. The advantage(s) must be specific. You can not be just a "good organization." You must be better at something specifically identifiable to your target audience than other organizations. So if you are "the best church for young families," for example, you must be able to back that up with some very specific things you do that are meaningful and valued by young families. What exactly makes you better than the other alternatives that your target audience will consider? Combining condition numbers 1, 2, and 3 together means you must be "really" good (not just in your

opinion) at something specific that you know to be valued highly by a particular group of people whom you wish to engage in some form of exchange.

4. The advantage(s) must be promotable, meaning you must be able to communicate the advantage to your target audience in language which they not only understand, but which is also highly motivating. The previous three characteristics must be present before this fourth characteristic has relevance, but unless this fourth point is implemented, the value of the first three goes wanting. Also implied in point number four is that you have a budget in place so that the competitive advantage can be promoted with enough frequency and reach to attract the target market audience. Since most religious organizations must rely more on personal communications rather than paid promotion methods, this point means that leaders must clearly and consistently communicate the competitive advantage to the organization's members and constituencies in internal messages that are easily and accurately passed along to target-market members via word-of-mouth. (*See* INTERNAL MARKETING.)

5. The advantage(s) should be sustainable, not transitory. Ideally, competitors should not easily copy the advantage(s). In some instances an organization can acquire such a well-entrenched image in the minds of the target audience that even if competitors copy the advantage it is still sustained in the eyes of the audience. An example of this in the commercial world is Wal-Mart's image as the low-cost retailer of consumer goods. Even if another competitor matches or beats Wal-Mart's prices Wal-Mart's image as the lower-cost provider could be sustained because it is so well-entrenched in the minds of consumers. Sustainability is a goal worthy of strategic thought by the religious organization even if it is elusive, simply because it continues to focus attention on the central question "Why should they *continue* to engage in exchange with us rather than another organization?"

REFERENCE

Cohen, William A., *The Marketing Plan* (New York: John Wiley & Sons), 1995.

SUGGESTED READING

Day, George S., *Market Driven Strategy* (New York: The Free Press), 1990.
Porter, Michael E., *Competitive Advantage* (New York: The Free Press), 1985.

CONSTITUENT ANALYSIS

A constituent is someone who works for, is a member of, attends, supports, or is affected by an organization. Constituent analysis refers to the process of analyzing the various constituent groups, which are related to or by a church or religious organization. One fundamental concept, which underlies this type of analysis, is that what is sometimes referred to as a market for a program or service is actually a composite of smaller markets, each with identifiable characteristics. When we speak of donor markets, for example, we are making reference to a large market, which is composed of smaller submarkets or segments. This market can be segmented in several ways to identify the various submarkets. The size of donations, for example, could be used to identify at least three submarkets or segments: large, average, and small.

This process of breaking up a market into smaller parts or segments is usually referred to as market segmentation. The basic premise is that the needs of constituents in one segment are different from those in another segment, and therefore different marketing strategies should be used to reach different segments. The results of the analysis should be an understanding of constituents' needs by segment and some insight into the types of strategies needed to meet those needs. This is the basis of the entire planning process if a constituent-oriented approach is to be used in planning.

For each segment that is identified, two basic questions must be asked: (1) What are the identifying characteristics of that segment? and (2) What is its size? Answering the first question helps define constituents' needs and helps develop a profile of constituents for each segment—the qualitative side of the market. The answer to the second question provides information on the size or quantitative side of the market. (*See* MARKET SEGMENTATION.)

CONSTITUENT BEHAVIOR

For the business firm, consumer behavior is the process involved when individuals or groups select, purchase, use, and dispose of goods, services, ideas, or experiences to satisfy their needs and desires (Solomon and Stuart, 2003). A church may refer to this process as constituent behavior. A marketer should understand the process that people go through when making choices and should also understand their needs and desires. Then, service offerings can be developed to satisfy those needs and desires.

For a person to attend church, one or more decisions must be made. Therefore, we should consider the decision-making process. This process is initiated when a person realizes that a difference exists between his or her current situation and a desired situation. That is, an individual recognizes that a problem exists. It may be that the individual feels an emptiness, a lack of purpose, or that something is missing in life. A parent may believe that a church is needed for guidance in a child's life.

Once the problem is noticed, the person or family may search for information about different alternatives that could be a solution to the problem. The search may involve looking in the yellow pages, asking friends about churches, searching the Internet, newspaper, or just driving around neighborhoods. A church's marketing may gain attention of those searching for information by a yellow page ad, Web site, signage, etc.

The alternative choices are evaluated, a decision is made, and attendance follows. These steps are followed by a postdecision process. Is the problem solved? Are the needs and desires satisfied? If so, a commitment is made and a relationship is developed. If not, another search may be initiated. A number of variables influence the decision-making process. Personal factors and environmental factors have an impact on decisions.

Personal factors include learning, perception, motivation, attitudes, personality, self-concept, age, life-cycle stage, occupation, economic situation, and lifestyle. Environmental factors are social influences such as culture, social values, norms, roles, social class, status, reference groups, family, and situational influences such as physical surroundings and time. All of these factors go into the deci-

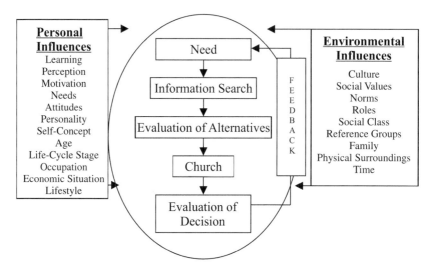

FIGURE 1. Simplified Version of Decision Process

sion of what church to attend. Church management should consider these variables when developing strategies and offerings.

The decision process is very complex. A simplified version is shown in Figure 1.

REFERENCE

Solomon, Michael R. and Elmore W. Stuart, *Marketing,* Third Edition (Upper Saddle River, NJ: Prentice Hall), 2003.

CONSTITUENT SERVICE

The 4 Ps of the marketing mix are promotion, place, price, and product. A product can be a tangible good, a service, or both. A product strategy should include the level of customer service. A church would refer to this service as constituent service. For a church to grow, it needs to attract new constituents and retain present constituents. Retention of present constituents is significantly influenced but the perceptions of the product (service) received by the constituents.

Organizations have long been concerned with delivery of a satisfactory level of constituent service, but it is safe to say that the level of concern has increased in recent years. Competitive forces and the more demanding nature of constituents have combined to put constituent service at, or near, the top of most marketers' list of important issues. Research indicates five dimensions used by constituents to define the quality of service they perceive they are receiving.

1. *Tangibles:* Appearance of physical facilities, equipment, personnel, and communications materials
2. *Reliability:* Ability to perform the promised service dependably and accurately
3. *Responsiveness:* Willingness to help customers and provide prompt service
4. *Assurance:* Knowledge and courtesy of employees and their ability to convey trust and confidence
5. *Empathy:* Caring, individualized attention the firm provides its customers (Zeithaml et al., 1990, p. 26)

Further research has revealed that while respondents rank all five toward the "very important" end of the scale in defining service quality, when asked, they said that reliability was the most critical. This result suggested that organizations must accomplish the following tasks with regard to their service strategy:

1. Determine the specific service expectations of the target market.
2. Design a service strategy grounded in meeting or exceeding those expectations.
3. Deliver on those promised service levels consistently when dealing with constituents.
4. If steps 1 through 3 are done better than competitors, a competitive advantage exists in the area of constituent service and should be exploited as such.

A vexing challenge for management, given the importance of reliability in defining service quality, is to close any gap that exists between expectations and ultimate delivery of service to constituents. Four service-related gaps should be of concern to marketing planners:

1. *Gap between constituents' expectations and management's perceptions.* Research into what constituents are actually thinking is needed; we cannot just assume what those expectations are without conducting the proper research.
2. *Gap between management perception and service quality specifications.* Knowledge of constituent expectations is but the first link in a chain of steps leading to constituent satisfaction with service delivery. Specifications of policies and tasks of service should be developed based on that knowledge, communicated to employees, and employees should know that their job performance will be based in part or in whole on meeting those specifications.
3. *Gap between service quality specifications and service delivery.* Highly motivated, trained, and well-informed employees are needed to actually perform the tasks specified as necessary for delivery of quality service. Control systems that are capable of measuring any gap between desired and actual service delivery should be in place to indicate where excellence or shortfalls are occurring.
4. *Gap between service delivery and external communication.* Excellent delivery of service specifications can still disappoint constituents if marketers have caused those constituents to have unrealistically high expectations of service. (Boyd et al., 1995, pp. 453-454)

In business, most customers who are dissatisfied do not complain. Instead, they search for alternatives and switch to another store (Richins, 1987, pp. 24-31). Therefore, management should carefully study customer satisfaction and dissatisfaction (Parasuraman et al., 1990, pp. 34-44). Churches should do the same thing, using a constituent satisfaction measurement program. Management tracks attitudes and feelings over time and develops program improvements as a result of the feedback. Get feedback by surveying people who have left the church. The information gathered can be useful in reducing future defections and possibly reattracting those who have defected.

A system should be developed for dealing with dissatisfaction. Helpful guidelines are as follows:

1. Make it easy for dissatisfaction to be expressed.
2. Conduct satisfaction research on a constituent basis.

3. Train employees to properly respond to dissatisfaction.
4. Respond quickly and minimize hardships when a problem does occur.
5. Evaluate complaints to pinpoint the core causes of dissatisfaction.
6. Identify patterns and opportunities for improvement for the future. (Berry and Parasuraman, 1991)

Satisfaction measurement is part of the concept of customer/constituent relationship management (CRM). CRM uses marketing to build long-term relationships with constituents to keep them satisfied and returning. Successful churches do a great job of getting constituents involved with the life of the church and getting the church involved with the lives of the constituents.

REFERENCES

Berry, Leonard L. and A. Parasuraman, *Marketing Services: Competing Through Quality* (New York: The Free Press), 1991.

Boyd Jr., Harper W., Orville C.Walker Jr., and Jean Claude Lerreche, *Marketing Management* (Chicago: Irwin), 1995, pp. 453-454.

Parasuraman, A., Leonard L. Berry, and Valarie A. Zeithaml, "Guidelines for conducting service quality research," *Marketing Research: A Magazine of Management and Applications,* (December 1990), pp. 34-44.

Richins, Marsha, "A Multivariate analysis of Response to Dissatisfaction," *Journal of the Academy of Marketing Science,* 15 (3), 1987, pp. 24-31.

Zeithaml, Valarie A., A. Parasuraman, and Leonard L. Berry, *Delivering Quality Service: Balancing Customer Perceptions and Expectations* (New York: The Free Press), 1990, p. 26.

CONTRIBUTION ANALYSIS

Contribution analysis refers to the process of breaking up total contributions to an organization into subgroups for greater details. A major problem for many churches and ministries is attracting a sufficient quantity of contributions to build *and* support the organization over a long period of time. This problem is faced by organizations just starting up, as well as established churches and ministries.

The total amount of charitable money raised by all organizations in 2004 was $249 billion. Over 76 percent of all contributions came from individuals, with the remainder coming from bequests, foundations and corporations. About 35 percent of every charity dollar goes to a church or religious organization. That amounted to $88 billion in 2004. About $1 out of every $3 was raised by mail or mail-assisted campaigns, and the rest by personal contact campaigns (Giving USA Foundation, 2005).

Fund-raising has passed through various stages of evolution— from begging, to collection, to campaigns, to development. Development, whereby the organization systematically builds up different classes of loyal donors who give consistently and receive benefits in the process of giving, is looked on by many as a more long-term approach to attracting funds.

REFERENCE

Giving USA Foundation, *Giving USA* (Indianapolis: Indiana University Center on Philanthropy), 2005.

CONTRIBUTION/COST CONTROLS

A contribution/cost control refers to the mechanisms an organization uses to manage these elements. Several tools are available for establishing cost control procedures, including budgets, expense ratios, and activity costs analysis. Budgets are a common tool used by most organizations for anticipating expense levels on a yearly basis. The budget is often established by using historical percentages of various expenses as a percent of sales. Thus, once the total level of expected contributions is established, expense items can be budgeted as a percent of total sales. If zero-based budgeting is used, the objectives to be accomplished must be specified and the expenditures necessary to accomplish these objectives estimated. The estimates are the budgeted expenses for the time period.

Contributions are controlled by tracing contributions on a weekly or at least a monthly basis. Many organizations have an annual drive for pledges, and others are continually seeking contributions from constituents. A prerequisite to controlling contributions is an annual projection of operating expenses. This projection, broken down on a quarterly or monthly basis, becomes the standard from which deviations are analyzed. For example, a church with a projected budget of $500,000 for the next fiscal year would be expecting about $125,000 per quarter, or $41,667 per month. If there were large variations related to certain times of the year, even the variations can be analyzed to determine the proportion of the budgeted amount given per month. If, historically, 20 percent of the budget were given during December, then 20 percent of next year's budget becomes the expected level of contributions to be used as the standard.

The same type of analysis used to control attendance can be used to analyze data on contributions. This type of analysis should be performed on a timely basis to enable expansion or cutbacks of programs when contribution levels go above or below the expected amounts for the period.

Once the budget is established, expense variance analysis by line item or expenditure category is used to control costs. Although it is not possible to establish standard costs for marketing expenditures, the budget amounts are the standards used to perform variance analysis. A typical procedure is to prepare monthly or quarterly budget reports showing the amount budgeted for the time period and the dollar and percentage variation from the budgeted amount, if any exists. Expenditure patterns that vary from the budgeted amounts are then analyzed to determine why the variations occurred.

Expense ratio analysis is another tool used to control costs. An important goal of every plan is to maintain the desired relationship between expenditures and results. Calculations of expense ratios provide information on what this relationship is at any time. Monthly, quarterly, and yearly ratio calculations should satisfy most administrators' needs for this type of data.

Common ratios are as follows:

1. Administrative expense ratio
2. Personal contacts expense ratio
3. Cost per personal contact
4. Promotion expense ratio

Many other financial ratios, such as percent of pledges given, percent pledging, etc., also provide measures that can be used to reduce or maintain cost levels.

Activity cost analysis is also very useful. This type of analysis permits evaluation of cost by individual activity, such as a fund-raising dinner. Analysis of these costs in relation to pledges produced is a key type of analysis for identifying effective and ineffective activities.

CONTRIBUTION SOURCES

Contribution sources are the various groups or organizations that contribute money. An organization can tap into a variety of sources for financial support. Some organizations often solicit funds primarily from one source—often wealthy individuals—to meet their financial needs. However, other sources include individuals, foundations, corporations, and government. Larger organizations solicit from all sources, and may make specific administrators responsible for each market. Ultimately, they seek to allocate the fund-raising budget in proportion to the giving potential of each donor market.

Individuals are the major sources of all charitable giving, accounting for some 83 percent of the total (Giving USA Foundation, 2005). Almost everyone in the nation contributes money to one or more organizations each year, the total amount varying with such factors as the giver's income, age, education, sex, ethnic background, and other characteristics. More money is contributed by high-income people in their middle years, and people of higher education. At the same time, giving levels vary substantially within each group. Some wealthy individuals give little and some lower-income individuals give a lot. Among wealthy people, for example, physicians tend to give less than lawyers (Giving USA Foundation, 2005).

Individual givers can be segmented into two broad groups: high-income givers and low-income givers. Although the large gifts of individuals often are the primary funds used in building programs, most churches and ministries count on small regular gifts for their operating budgets. The small gifts of $5 to $20 per month given to ministries usually account for the major portion of their contributions in any given year. Churches count on the regular tithes and offerings of members for their financial base.

Over 26,000 foundations in the United States are set up to give money to worthwhile causes. They fall into the following groups:

1. *Family foundations* are wealthy individuals who support a limited number of activities of interest to the founders. Decisions tend to be made by family members and/or a board of advisors.
2. *General Christian foundations* support a wide range of church/mission activities and are usually run by a permanent staff.
3. *Corporate foundations* are corporations permitted to give away up to 5 percent of the corporation's adjusted gross income.
4. *Community trusts,* found in cities or regions, are usually small foundations whose funds are pooled.

With the large number of foundations, the fund-raiser must know how to locate the few that would be the most likely to support a given project or cause. The Foundation Center, a nonprofit organization with research centers in New York, Washington, and Chicago, collects and distributes information on foundations. In addition, many libraries around the country also carry important materials describing foundations. The most important materials are:

1. *The Foundation Grants Index,* which lists the grants that have been given in the past year by foundation, subject, state, and other groupings.
2. *The Foundation Directory,* which lists over 2,500 foundations that either have assets of over $1 million or award grants of more than $500,000 annually.
3. *The Foundation News,* which is published six times a year by the Council on Foundations and describes new foundations, new funding programs, and changes in existing foundations.
4. *Fund Raising Management,* which is a periodical publishing articles on fund-raising management.

The key problem in dealing with foundations is that of matching. The organization should search for foundations matched to its interests. After identifying a few foundations whose interests might match your needs, you should try to qualify their level of interest before investing a lot of time in preparing the paperwork required by most foundations. Most are willing to respond to a letter of inquiry, phone call, or personal visit regarding how interested they are likely to be in a project.

Churches or ministries with schools or community outreach programs are often awarded grants to develop new programs or buy special equipment. One Christian school administrator was able to get a $50,000 grant from a foundation to buy personal computers for the school. Another ministry was able to get a grant from a relief foundation to purchase a building to feed and house "street people."

Business organizations represent another distinct source of funds. Corporations have been especially supportive of youth-oriented activities, and many larger cities have a *Christian Business Directory* or yellow pages that lists businesses owned by Christians.

Corporations can make more different types of gifts than foundations. A business firm may give money, furniture, food products, clothing, or services. An organization may be able to use corporate facilities such as an auditorium or camp facilities for a nominal fee simply by asking.

Other sources of funds are government agencies at the federal, state, and local levels that are able to make grants to worthwhile causes. For example, a ministry in El Paso, Texas, was able to get a grant to build and operate a facility to house and feed illegal immigrants until they could be processed and deported to their home country. While there, of course, they were asked to participate in chapel services and Bible studies given in Spanish. The ministry staff ran the facility and was paid through the grant.

Other government agencies also make grants to support health care as well as university teaching and research. Christian colleges and other ministries can use these grants to carry out specific projects.

REFERENCE

Giving USA Foundation, *Giving USA* (Indianapolis: Indiana University Center on Philanthropy), 2005.

CONTROLLING MARKETING ACTIVITIES

Many organizations fail to understand the importance of establishing procedures to monitor and control the marketing process—a failing that leads to less than optimal performance. Control should be a natural follow-through in developing a plan. No plan should be considered complete until controls are identified and the procedures for recording and transmitting control information to administrators are established.

Planning and control should be integral processes. In fact, planning can be defined as a process that includes establishing a system for feedback of results. This feedback reflects the organization's performance in reaching its objectives through implementation of the marketing plan. The relationship between planning and control is depicted in Figure 2.

The planning process results in a specific plan being developed for a program and/or service. This plan is implemented (marketing activities are performed in the manner described in the plan) and results are produced. These results are attendance, contributions, and accompanying constituent attitudes, preferences, and behaviors. Information on these results and other related factors are given to administrators, who compare the results with objectives to evaluate performance. This performance evaluation identifies the areas where decisions must be made. The actual decision making controls the plan by altering it to accomplish stated objectives and a new cycle begins. The information flows are the key to a good control system. Deciding what information is provided to which managers in what time periods is the essence of a control system.

The long-run marketing plan is composed of many short-run plans. An economist once noted that "We plan in the long run but live in the

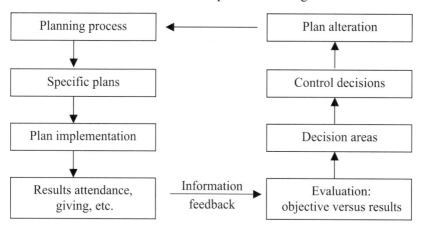

FIGURE 2. Planning and Control Model

short run." If each of our short-run plans is controlled properly, the long-run plans are more likely to be controlled. The administrator cannot afford to wait for the time period of a plan to pass before control information is available. The information must be available within a time frame, which is long enough to allow results to accrue, but short enough to allow actions to align results with objectives. Although some types of organizations may find weekly or bimonthly results necessary, most organizations can adequately control operations with monthly or quarterly reports. Cumulative monthly or quarterly reports become annual reports, which in turn become the feedback needed to control the plan.

COSTS TO TARGET AUDIENCE

By "costs" we are referring to those sacrifices that are incurred by members of the target audience in order to obtain the offering of the religious organization, not the monetary expenses incurred by the organization (*see* EXCHANGE). In an exchange process between two parties both must have something valued by the other party and be willing to give that "something" in exchange for what the other party has that is valued. The something the target audience gives up is, therefore, a cost to them of engaging in exchange with the religious organization. These people face four types of costs, as follows:

1. *Economic costs* (e.g., to give up money or goods as tithes or offerings, or simply to buy a product or service)
2. *Sacrifices of old ideas, values, or views of the world* (e.g., to give up believing that women are inferior, that abortion is not sin, that God is vindictive, that one cannot be forgiven)
3. *Sacrifices of old patterns of behavior* (e.g., to start a daily devotional or attend church services regularly)
4. *Sacrifices of time and energy* (e.g., to perform a voluntary service or give blood to a church blood drive)

In return for these types of sacrifices, consumers of ecclesial services receive benefits of three basic kinds: *goods and services, social,* and *psychological.* The combination of these kinds of sacrifices and benefits yield the matrix outlined in Table 2.

TABLE 2. Cost Benefit for Religious Organizational Exchanges

	Benefits			
Costs	A Good	A Service	Social	Psychological
Give up economic assets	Buy a tape of sermons	Church school education	Donate to building fund	Church tithes and offerings
Give up old ideas, values, opinions	Receive free clothing donated by church members	Premarital counseling, marriage counseling	Prison ministry by laypersons	God can be trusted, sins can be forgiven
Give up old behaviors, undertake or learn new behaviors	Stay drug free and receive a "how-to" videotape	Participate in stop smoking program, home budget counseling	Go to divorce recovery group once a week	Start daily devotion, attend church services
Give up time or energy	Come to revival meetings and get a free bible	Attend a free religious concert	Volunteer for vacation Bible school	Give blood in church blood drive

An increased understanding of the nature of perceived costs from the perspective of the target audience will aid the religious organization marketers seeking to enhance the prospects of exchange. Marketers who focus primarily on informing the target audience of the benefits from the exchange may fail to motivate many people in the target audience. They might acknowledge the benefits' existence and value, but fear incurring the costs more than they desire the benefits. Understanding the target audience's perception of costs requires research by the organization. It may be discovered, for example, that the perceived costs incurred by someone asked to say the prayers at the main church service include

- Fear that they cannot pray as well in public as other church members
- Worry that they will forget parts of the prayer they planned to say or will repeat themselves
- Concern that they will mispronounce the names of ill church members who requested special prayers
- Embarrassment that their clothes are not attractive enough to be seen on the platform
- Fear that the prayer will be seen as too short or too long

And so on. By understanding all the costs incurred in any exchange marketers can try to find ways to minimize them, provide a means of "subsidizing" them, and show that the organization is sympathetic to the person's concerns with incurring the costs. In this way the organization can put both benefits and costs in a context that increases the likelihood of exchange occurring.

SUGGESTED READING

Lovelock, Christopher H. and Charles B. Weinberg, *Public and Nonprofit Marketing,* Second Edition (Redwood City, CA: The Scientific Press), 1989.

DATA COLLECTION

Data collection refers to the process of obtaining data from those individuals or organizations selected to be included in a sample. This involves several related decisions. The first choice is between observation and interrogation, and the second choice is which specific observation or interrogation technique to use. These decisions, in turn, depend on what information is needed, from which sample elements, in what time frame and at what level of cost.

Data collection can be the single most costly element in a project or it can be of low relative cost, depending on the nature of the project. However, data collection is always an important determinant of research value because of the influence of the conditions surrounding data collection on the validity of the results obtained.

The most common data-collection techniques are self-administered questionnaires, telephone interviews, and personal interviews. The Internet can also be used to collect data. Each of these techniques has advantages and disadvantages and can be evaluated on speed, costs, sample size, accuracy, and reliability.

DATA COLLECTION AND ANALYSIS

Data collection and analysis refers to the tools and techniques used to turn data into meaningful information. The major criterion is the nature of the data to be analyzed. The purpose of the analysis is to obtain meaning from the raw data that have been collected.

The analysis can be formal or informal. Informal analysis would involve looking through responses or databanks made by constituents. However, this can produce bias and also is impractical when large amounts of data are to be analyzed. Formal analysis usually involves the use of analytical tools such as statistics, to summarize and test the data.

Once the data are collected and analyzed, the researcher must interpret the results of the findings in terms of the problem studied. This means determining what the results imply about the solution to the problem and recommending a course of action to solve it. If the purpose of the research project was to determine the feasibility of introducing a new program and the results of the research project show that the program will produce an acceptable level of attendance, then the researcher should recommend introduction of the program unless known internal or external barriers cannot be overcome.

The researcher must move beyond the role of the scientist in objectively collecting and analyzing data. Now the role is as a consultant in a framework that states: "Given these facts and this interpretation, I recommend this action." This does not, of course, mean that the action recommended will be pursued by the organization. The researcher usually only makes recommendations. Other administrators have the prerogative of accepting or rejecting the recommendations. However, the researcher must still recommend the action. Failure to do this is analogous to a dog chasing a car—the dog would not know what to do with the car once he caught it.

DATABASE OR DONORBASE MARKETING

True database marketing creates customer intelligence that contributes to the development of effective constituent relationships. Database marketing is an organizational process that is customer research-driven. The information base is dynamic and evolving, preferably with two-way dialog with the customer. This measure of the importance of creating and maintaining a good database of market information is what *Business Week* devoted the cover story of its September 5, 1994, issue to, calling it "one of the biggest changes in marketing since 'new and improved'" ("Databased Marketing," 1994, p. 56). Since that time the concept of database marketing, coupled with new technologies, has grown to the point that a new generation of marketing professionals has been created. These new database marketing professionals offer skills in four primary areas:

1. *Secondary data acquisition,* including analysis of the value of lists
2. *Database building,* including the understanding of computer hardware and software,
3. *Target marketing,* including maximizing database record use
4. *One-to-one marketing,* managing and refining the targeting process to customize contacts for every constituent

The popularity of database marketing is grounded in the belief that marketing planning begins by understanding the customer—his or her buying and consumption patterns, location, interest, and other aspects of buying behavior discernable from databases—and then formulating plans that attempt to weave the firm's product or service into the consumer's pattern of behavior. The basic idea behind use of databases is, "If that is what consumers are doing, how can we make them want to do that more often and with our product?" This approach to satisfying customers adheres to the belief that the best indicator of future behavior is past behavior.

When applied to an organization's donor base, this concept can track donors through their lifecycle of giving to an organization and help determine what most appeals to various donor groups. Larger religious organizations have used this concept for years to help build a base of constituents who interact with the organization is some way. The interaction may be through the mail, by telephone, e-mail, or attendance at events or services provided by the organization. The process of data collection and manipulation, which allows such powerful tactical marketing actions to occur, consists of several steps:

1. *Constituent action.* The process begins with constutients taking some form of action—they attend an event, send a letter or e-mail, they telephone, or order a product. This behavior may be combined with other information to identify a broad profile of each constituent in the database.
2. *Digesting the data.* Sophisticated statistical techniques are used to merge data on the consumer into a coherent, consolidated database. Other software allows the marketer to "drill down" into the data to reveal patterns of behavior for classes of constituents.
3. *Profiling the ideal constituent.* Neural networks that "learn" from the data are used to identify a model constituent (i.e., the common characteristics held by the high-donor constituents). This allows the marketer to find constituents or potential constituents who share those characteristics in common with the high donor.
4. *Using the knowledge.* This data can be used in many ways: determine who gets which mailouts, to develop attributes for new services with a targeted list of constituents, for new service/product introduction announcements, and to tailor ad messages and target them by constituent group, etc.

Modern technology has made it possible for marketers to do extensive searches through a large database, essentially mining the data. Data mining is the process of sorting through the data to find hidden patterns, potential trends, and correlations between constituents, or within a single constituent's data. Data mining is predominantly accomplished through mathematical and statistical processes and is typically done utilizing software developed for this purpose.

Although modern technology, including neural network software and parallel processor hardware, makes the use of such database marketing possible, it is old-fashioned objectives that drive the interest in databases—marketers are seeking to know their constituents so well that they can anticipate their needs and provide those products and services to constituents before they even know they want them. This is relationship marketing at its most efficient evolutionary stage. Computer technology allows the marketer to acquire knowledge of the purchasing habits of millions of individual constituents and to "weave relationships" with them by anticipating their needs and informing them of need—satisfying products specifically suited to their situation. To some degree, the marketing plans of companies actively engaged in database marketing are driven by the desire to maximize the use of their databases and the technology that allows manipulation of those databases. In other words, the ability to use the database in certain ways means those uses will become the implementation of the marketing plan (i.e., the plan conforms to fit the technology available). This is not necessarily an inappropriate or "backward" approach to marketing as long as marketers do not lose sight of the fact that the ultimate goal of any use of technology or objective of a marketing plan is to identify how you can gain a competitive advantage in satisfying constituents' needs and wants.

Jackson and Wang (1995) identified fifteen ways to use a marketing database. Many of these concepts can be applied to church and religious organizations. The concepts are listed here to illustrate the spectrum of possibilities for the use of databases in data-based marketing planning.

1. Identify your best customers.
2. Develop new customers.
3. Deliver a message consistent with product usage.
4. Reinforce consumer purchase decisions.
5. Cross-sell and complementary-sell products.
6. Apply three-tiered communications.
7. Improve delivery of sales promotion.
8. Refine the marketing process.
9. Increase the effectiveness of distribution-channel marketing.
10. Maintain equity.
11. Establish a management resource.
12. Take advantage of stealth communications.
13. Conduct customer, product, and marketing research.
14. Personalize customer service.
15. Provide program synergy and integration.

REFERENCES

"Databased Marketing," *Business Week,* September 5, 1994, pp. 56-62.

Jackson, Rob and Paul Wang, *Strategic Database Marketing* (Lincolnwood: NTC Publishing Group), 1995.

DEMOGRAPHICS

Demographics are statistical characteristics of the human population. These observable characteristics can be personal, economic, and social. Examples are age, gender, income, occupation, race, education, religion, marital status, family size, age of children, home ownership, and residence location.

Demographics help in understanding and assessing a market and in developing marketing strategy. These quantifiable factors are good predictors of behavior and therefore can be used as a way to segment a market. In fact, demographic segmentation is the most common type of segmentation. Demography can help in identifying potential customers and selecting target markets. The knowledge of statistical characteristics can serve as a basis for advertising decisions such as what appeal and media to use.

The marketer's use of demographics is based on the thought that people with different characteristics have different needs. A church can create methods of worship and programs to meet the needs of individual demographic groups. A church may build a strong youth program if it has a membership composed of many large young families. A strong youth program would also appeal to nonmember parents with young kids.

Demographic data are widely available. The United States Department of Commerce provides information through the U.S. Census Bureau. This source is available at the Web site, www.census.gov, and is available in many public libraries. Private companies such as Claritas (www.claritas.com) and ESRI, Inc. (www.esri.com) also provide demographic information and many other services.

DESCRIPTIVE (QUANTITATIVE) RESEARCH

Descriptive research, sometimes referred to as quantitative research, is one of three types of research designs (*see* EXPLORATORY, descriptive, and causal).

As the name implies, descriptive research seeks to *describe* something. More specifically, descriptive research is conducted when seeking to accomplish the following objectives:

1. Describe the characteristics of relevant groups such as the 20 percent of our supporters who generate 80 percent of our donations.
2. Determine the extent to which two or more variables covary. For example, does interest in our programs vary by age of respondent?
3. Estimate the proportion of a population who act or think a certain way. For example, how often do childless couples attend church in a typical month?
4. Make specific predictions. For example, we might want to forecast the number of people who would attend an early morning prayer service.

Descriptive research is highly structured and rigid in its approach to data collection compared to exploratory research's unstructured and flexible approach. As such, descriptive research presupposes much prior knowledge on the part of the researcher regarding

who will be targeted as a respondent,
what issues are of highest priority to be addressed in the study,
how the questions are to be phrased to reflect the vocabulary and experience of the respondents,
when to ask the questions,
where to find the respondents, and
why these particular questions need to be answered in order to make decisions.

Thus, exploratory research may often be needed to allow descriptive research requirements to be met.

The best known and most frequently used descriptive design, cross-sectional analysis, involves a SAMPLING of a population of interest at one point in time. This technique is sometimes referred to as a *sample survey,* because it often involves a probability sampling plan intended to choose respondents who will be representative of a certain population. As with all descriptive research, sample surveys are characterized by a high degree of structure—in both the data-collection instrument and in the data-collection process itself. The only way we can be sure we are measuring frequency or variation in the phenomenon under investigation is to build a high degree of structure into the instrument and process. That structure was *not* needed in exploratory research. It would have been a deterrent to achieving our objectives of insight, ideas, hypotheses, clarification, etc.

Cross-sectional surveys do not always have to involve selection of a one-time sample of respondents from the population. Several firms such as The Home Testing Institute, Market Facts, and National Family Opinion (NFO) operate omnibus panels that consist of hundreds of thousands of U.S. households that have been selected to proportionately represent the U.S. population along key dimensions such as age, income, sex, ethnic composition, and geographic dispersion. Members of such households are recruited to serve on the panel and agree to participate in answering questionnaires or trying products when requested to do so by the company maintaining the panel. Using such a panel allows an organization to select certain demographic characteristics for respondents (e.g., single males under age thirty-five) and send a questionnaire to them, knowing that the cost of finding and getting a response from a targeted number of this group (e.g., 1,000 completed questionnaires) is much less than trying to complete such a project in the general population where response rates may be as low as 1 or 2 percent.

These panels are particularly cost-effective when research is being conducted on a topic where the incidence rate in the population is very low (e.g., vegetarians, people with three-car garages, people with home movie theaters, etc.). In such cases it is possible to buy a few screening questions on the monthly questionnaire sent to, say, 50,000 panel members to identify those members who fit the desired profile, then send only those qualified panelists a longer questionnaire to obtain the detailed information being sought. Firms maintaining such omnibus panels turn over membership frequently to avoid participating households becoming "professional respondents," which would reduce the respondents' representativeness for the general population. (*See also* QUESTIONNAIRE and SAMPLING.)

SUGGESTED READING

Wrenn, Bruce, Robert Stevens, and David Loudon, *Marketing Research* (Binghamton, NY: The Haworth Press), 2002.

DIRECT MARKETING

The business definition of direct marketing is "any direct communication to consumer or business recipient that is designed to generate a response in the form of an order, a request for further information, and /or a visit to a store or other place of business for purchase of a product" (Direct Marketing Association, 2002). This is sometimes referred to as direct-response marketing, direct-response retailing, direct-response advertising, direct-response promotion, and nonstore retailing.

For a church, direct marketing is simply the direct communication with a member or a potential member in an effort to generate a response or visit. The communication may be by mail, telephone, person-to-person, direct-response television, the Internet, or any combination of these methods.

Direct marketing has several advantages, depending upon the method of communication contacts can be made efficiently and relatively inexpensively. Potential members can be targeted and specifically pinpointed, and the contact can be personalized. Also, recipients can respond at a time that is convenient to them. Direct marketing has its disadvantages. Often, a low response rate can lead to a higher cost per response. Another problem is clutter. For example, because so much direct mail is sent, many pieces are never opened. Although some people have a low opinion of direct marketers, a long-term growth is projected for direct marketing.

A comprehensive up-to-date database of potential contacts is extremely important for direct marketing. Names, addresses, telephone numbers, and background data should be collected, stored, and used in an appropriate manner. Experienced personnel, current technology, and good equipment are needed to adequately manage the database.

REFERENCE

Direct Marketing Association, "What Is Direct Marketing," Accessed at www.the-dma.org/aboutdma/whatisthedma.shtml#whatis.

ENVIRONMENTAL SCANNING

Environmental factors can have a substantial impact on marketing and on the managing of an organization. Therefore, marketers should monitor developments, trends, and changes in the environment.

Environmental scanning is "the process of collecting information about the external marketing environment in order to identify and interpret potential trends" (Boone and Kurtz, 2002, p. 41). It involves identifying those realities in a church's operating sphere that directly or indirectly influence its plans and operations. Environmental information can be helpful in decision making, as this information can lead to seizing opportunities or dodging threats.

A church's operating sphere includes economic, technological, cultural, social, legal, political, competitive, and organizational environments. The most important point a manager can learn from an analysis of environmental factors is the answer the following question: "How do these factors influence marketing plans being developed or precipitate changes in an existing plan?" The answer involves keeping in tune with the operating environment and relating environmental changes to the planning process. Managers continually need to ask themselves two basic questions: "Are we doing the right things?" and "Are we doing things right?" The first question is concerned with direction and adaptation, or keeping in the mainstream of what is going on in the worlds in which we operate. The second question is concerned with effectiveness and efficiency.

Some environmental factors are relatively easy to identify and consider when developing strategy. For example, suppose that a church in a small town decided that it would increase its membership by purchasing a new pipe organ. The decision was made to build the whole organization's marketing thrust around its music program and the new organ. They decided to include a drawing of the organ in the church's logo. Then, they got the news that a large corporation is closing its local operations in their town and transferring its employees (who comprise 40 percent of the church's membership) to other cities. This environmental impact would be so severe that the church probably would be wise not to go into debt to finance the organ. Perhaps their marketing efforts should be changed or adapted in response to changing environmental realities.

Of course, environmental factors and trends are not always so easy to recognize. Since the environment is so large and complex, a manager must establish a standard of relevance in the analysis, which means developing an approach to determine whether or not an environmental factor is important to the church. This approach can be accomplished by developing a list of words that can be used as a focus when shifting through various sources of information. In developing a list of key words or phrases, and in the information search stage, a basic question continually should be asked, "Could this factor directly or indirectly influence our market or marketing strategy?" If the answer is "yes," the factor is examined. If the answer is "no," the factor is omitted. This question is the standard of relevance used to judge the importance of various environmental factors.

REFERENCE

Boone, Louis E. and David L. Kurtz, *Contemporary Marketing* (South-Western Thomson Learning), 2002, p. 41.

EXCHANGE

The concept of exchange helps us to understand how a religious organization can fulfill its mission by interacting with various targeted publics. For an exchange to occur between two or more parties (e.g., between a religious organization and an individual, or between two organizations), all parties must have something of value (SOV) in the eyes of another party and be willing to exchange that SOV for the other party's SOV. This exchange of SOV's can be graphically depicted as follows:

SOV: Product   SOV: Response

A religious organization's products can consist of:

Goods: literature, etc.
Services: counseling, etc.
Persons: speakers, etc.
Places: spiritual retreat center, etc.
Organization: youth club, etc.
Activities: musical performance, etc.
Ideas: pro-life, etc.

The individual or organization's response can consist of:

Financial resources: money, etc.
Another product: providing a service, etc.
A social behavior: the performance of some desirable activity or nonperformance of some undesirable activity.
Acceptance or adoption: of an idea, value, or view of the world.

Not all of the interaction between a religious organization and its publics can be characterized as exchange (e.g., sharing the gospel, disaster relief, etc., are not exchanges), but it is safe to say that virtually all religious organizations must successfully manage some exchange processes to attract the resources needed for survival and/or to achieve their fundamental mission. Marketers believe that the exchange process is at the core of what defines marketing itself. Witness the American Marketing Association's definition of marketing: "The process of planning and executing the conception, pricing, promoting, and distribution of ideas, goods, and services *to create exchanges* that satisfy individual and organizational objectives" (emphasis added; Nichols, 1985, p. 1).

To give a sense of how an exchange framework can be used in the development of a marketing strategy, suppose a church school administrator seeks to persuade a couple who have recently joined the congregation to send their seven-year-old son to the church's elementary day school, instead of sending him to public school. We could represent this situation in the following way:

The SOV of the parents desired by the school:

1. Parents' acceptance of the importance of religious-based education
2. Child's enrollment in school
3. Tuition

The parents in turn hope to satisfy certain desires by the school's education. We could diagram these as follows:

The SOV of the school desired by the parents:

1. Training in values and religious beliefs
2. Education in academic subjects exceeding that of public schools
3. Healthy, safe environment
4. Socialization with other "quality" children

It would be helpful for the administrator to know the relative importance parents attach to each of these wants. Many religious organizations adopt a selling or product orientation that assumes everyone will recognize the obvious and inherent value of their product. This is an *inside-out* perspective. In contrast, a MARKETING ORIENTATION always takes an *outside-in* perspective by looking at the congregation's programs and ministries from the perspective of the other party (the consumer). We may think that the value of religious education is real, significant, and obvious, but if parents do not perceive its value *as they define value,* or if this value does not equal or exceed the value of what they must offer in response, then exchange will not take place.

Elaborating the Exchange Process

We have examined the exchange process as if it involved only two parties. But an exchange process may involve multiple parties. We can illustrate a multiple-party exchange process by introducing the child into our example. Three sets of wants and/or values being considered in the exchange process are shown in Figure 3.

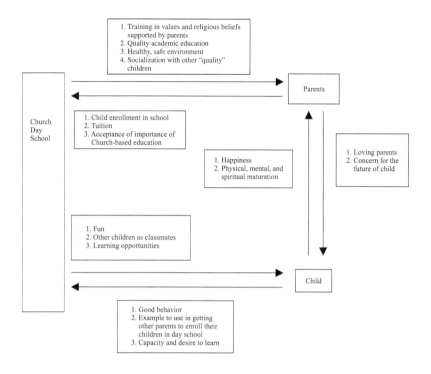

FIGURE 3. Three-Party Exchange Map Showing Want Vectors

The child wants to feel loved and cared for by the parents, including parental concern for doing what is good for the child in the long-run. *The school* is looking for children who have the capacity and desire to learn, who will be well-behaved, and who can be used as examples of the type of children enrolled in the day school. The church values this type of student in order to encourage other parents to enroll their children in its school. *The parents* want a happy, well-adjusted child with the values and beliefs they prize, as well as an academic training that prepares the child for further education.

Not included in the diagram, but still pertinent parties to the three-way exchange, would be, on the school's side, accrediting associations and other agencies that could affect the parents' perception of the value of the school's program. On the parents' side would be other institutions, such as financial institutions, that might affect the parents' financial ability to enroll their child in the day school. Clearly the church, as marketer, must take these various needs and weightings of value into consideration when formulating strategies to attract students to its school.

When marketers are anxious to consummate a transaction, they may be tempted to exaggerate the actual product benefits. Thus the administrator may be tempted to overstate the competence of the teachers or understate the total costs to the parents, financial and otherwise. By doing so, he or she may succeed in getting the parents to enroll their child, but the parents and/or child will become dissatisfied because of the difference between their *expectations* and the school's *performance*. As unhappy participants in this exchange, they can be expected to complain a great deal, talk negatively about the school to other parents or playmates, or leave the school and church. In the case of the day school, these dissatisfactions could carry over into other exchanges between the church and the family.

The best transactions are those in which it is realized that both (or all) parties are not simply seeking a single transaction but a continuing expected behavior on the part of the other party, and where parties behave in such a way as to ensure the other will receive the expected values from the exchange.

This exchange scenario merely illustrates one of many exchange relationships that religious organizations may be required to effectively manage in order to achieve organizational goals. As this example shows, conceptualizing the interaction between the organization and its various targeted publics as exchanges provides a framework for developing marketing strategy. How can the organization effectively build in value (from the exchange partner's perspective), and effectively communicate that value to establish an exchange relationship? Are there ways that the organization can help their exchange partner's exchanges with other parties (e.g., the parents with their child) become more successful, and thus enhance the other party's overall satisfaction with the organization? Such strategic thinking is not only conducive to better marketing success, but also achieves the higher goals of making a positive different in the lives of people—a goal common to virtually all religious organizations.

REFERENCE

Nichols, William G., "AMA Board Approves of New Marketing Definition," *Marketing News,* 19 (March 1), 1985, p. 1.

SUGGESTED READING

Bagozzi, Richard P., "Marketing As Exchange," *American Behavioral Scientist,* (March-April), 1978, pp. 535-556.
Lee, Richard R., "Religious Practice As Social Exchange: An Explanation of the Empirical Findings," *Sociological Analysis,* 53 (1), 1992, pp. 1-35.

EXPLORATORY (QUALITATIVE) RESEARCH

Exploratory research, sometimes referred to as qualitative research, is one of three types of RESEARCH DESIGNS: EXPLORATORY, DESCRIPTIVE, and causal.

Exploratory research is in some ways akin to detective work. It involves a search for "clues" to reveal what happened or is currently taking place. A variety of sources might be used to provide insights and information, and the researcher/detective "follows where his or her nose leads" in the search for ideas, insights, and clarification. Researchers doing exploratory research must adopt a very flexible attitude toward collecting information in this type of research and be constantly asking themselves what lies beneath the surface of what they are learning and/or seeing. An insatiable curiosity is a valuable trait for exploratory researchers.

Such curiosity will serve the exploratory researcher well when, for example, he or she sees the need to ask a follow-up question of a respondent who has mentioned some unanticipated answer to a researcher's query. The follow-up question is not listed on the researcher's interview guide, but the curious interviewer instinctively knows that the conversation should begin to deviate from the guide because the unexpected response may be revealing much more important issues surrounding the topic for investigation than were originally anticipated by the researcher. A willingness to follow one's instincts and detour into new territory is not only acceptable in exploratory research, but commendable! Inspired insight, new ideas, clarifications, and revelatory observations are all the desired outcomes from exploratory research and decision makers should not judge the quality of the idea or insight based on its source.

Although we do not want to give the impression that any approach is acceptable for doing exploratory research, or that all methods are of equal value in providing desired information, exploratory research is characterized by a flexibility of method that is minimal with other research design types.

Exploratory research is needed whenever the decision maker has the following objectives:

1. More precisely defining an ambiguous problem or opportunity
2. Increasing the decision maker's understanding of an issue
3. Developing hypotheses that could explain the occurrence of certain phenomena
4. Generating ideas
5. Providing insights
6. Establishing priorities for future research or determining the practicality of conducting some research
7. Identifying the variables and levels of variables for descriptive or causal research

Tools Used to Conduct Exploratory Research

Literature Review

More often than not the proper place to begin a research study is to investigate previous work related to the research issues under study. Exploratory research seeks to generate ideas, insights, and hypotheses, and reading what others have done and discovered about the topic in which you are interested can save valuable time and resources in the search for those ideas.

Personal Interviews

One of the best ways to obtain desired insights, hypotheses, clarifications, etc., is to talk with someone whose experience, expertise, or position gives him or her unique perspective on the subject of interest. The key to achieving your research objective of gaining insight, ideas, etc., through exploratory personal interviews is to be flexible and think about what you are hearing.

Researchers should never confuse the exploratory personal interview with one conducted in descriptive research. Descriptive-research interviewing requires a consistency in the questions asked and the way the questions are asked which is not conducive to achieving exploratory objectives. With exploratory interviewing, we are not trying to precisely measure some variable, we are trying to gain penetrating insights into some important issue. Hence, each of our exploratory interviews may take a different tack as we seek to probe and query each key informant to gain full benefit of their unique experiences.

Focus Groups

One of the most popular techniques for conducting exploratory research are FOCUS GROUPS, a small number of people (usually eight to twelve) convened to address topics introduced by a group moderator. The moderator works from a topic outline developed with input from moderator, researcher, and decision maker. Focus groups have proven to be of particular value in the following:

- Allowing researchers to see how their subjects act, think, and respond to the organization's efforts
- Generating hypotheses that can be tested by descriptive or causal research
- Giving respondent impressions of new programs
- Suggesting the current temperament of a target audience
- Making abstract data "real"—such as seeing how a "strongly agree" response on a survey appears in the faces and demeanor of "real" people

Focus groups are popular because they not only are an efficient, effective means of achieving these goals but also because decision makers can attend them, observing the responses of the participants "live." This observation can be a double-edged sword, for while it does make the abstract "real," it can deceive the novice into believing that the entire audience is represented by the respondents in the focus group. Conducting more focus groups to see a larger number of respondents does not convert the exploratory findings into descriptive data. Focus groups are one of several means of achieving the objectives of exploratory research and should not be overused or believed to be generating results that were never the intent of this technique.

Analysis of Selected Cases

Another means of achieving the objectives of exploratory research is to conduct in-depth analysis of selected cases of the subject under investigation. This approach is of particular value when a complex set of variables may be at work in generating observed results and intensive study is needed to unravel the complexities. Here again, the exploratory investigator is best served by an active curiosity and willingness to deviate from the initial plan when findings suggest new courses of inquiry might prove more productive. The exploratory research objectives of generating insights and hypotheses would be well served by use of this technique.

Projective Techniques

Researchers might be exploring a topic in which respondents are either unwilling or unable to directly answer questions about why they think or act as they do. Highly sensitive topics involving their private lives are obviously in this category, but more mundane behaviors may also hide deep psychological motivations. The method used to uncover these hidden motives is one of the so-called projective techniques, named because respondents project their deep psychological motivations through a variety of communication and observable methods.

One must be skilled not only in structuring these approaches, but also must be an experienced professional in interpreting the results. Although shown to provide intriguing new insights into behavior, they are best left to experts to operate and interpret.

SUGGESTED READING

Wrenn, Bruce, Robert Stevens, and David Loudon, *Marketing Research: Text and Cases* (Binghamton, NY: The Haworth Press), 2002.

FACILITY DESIGN

Churches and ministries have to make decisions on the design of their facilities because this can affect constituents' attitudes and behavior. Consider how the "atmosphere" of a church can affect constituents. Many older churches have gothic designs with drab wall colors that may create a cold, unfriendly feeling, especially among visitors. Newer facilities can be designed with colors, textures, furnishings, and layouts to reinforce positive feelings of warmth, openness, etc.

An organization that is designing a service facility for the first time faces four major design decisions:

1. *What should the building look like on the outside?* The building can look like a Greek temple, a villa, a glass skyscraper, or another genre. It can look awe-aspiring, ordinary, or intimate.
2. *How should the building be laid out?* The rooms and corridors must be designed to handle capacity crowds so that people do not have to experience congestion.
3. *What should the building feel like on the inside?* Every building conveys a feeling, whether intended or unplanned; awesome and somber, bright and modern, or warm and intimate. Each feeling will have a different effect on visitors and their overall satisfaction with the facility.
4. *What materials would best support the desired feeling of the building?* The feeling of a building is conveyed by color, brightness, size, shape, volume, pitch, scent, freshness, softness, smoothness, and temperature. The planners must choose colors, fabrics, and furnishings that create or reinforce the desired feeling.

Each facility will have a look that may add to or detract from constituent satisfaction and staff performance. Since the staff must work in the facility all day long, the facility should be designed to support them in performing their work with ease and cheerfulness. Many of the decisions discussed in this section require outside assistance.

The selection of building color, for example, is a task for the expert designer, not the layperson. Color is a highly technical subject, and, when approached from the lay point of view, choice may be influenced by the preferences of the individual. Sometimes those colors that we personally like or feel would be suitable are incompatible with wall texture or atmosphere.

People are known to react significantly to certain colors and their combinations. As a result, appropriately color-coordinated buildings attract better responses than do those with hit-or-miss color schemes. The color of a building or walls can make people feel that it is weak or strong, dirty or clean, heavy or light, and even masculine or feminine.

Modern buildings use intensive fluorescent illumination ranging upwards from fifty-foot candles. Colors must be designed with lighting in mind. When the same color is viewed under incandescent light, the colors appear to change.

This discussion should point out the need for the use of assistance in building design, color selection, etc. This assistance does come with a price, but in the long run it is easier to do things right the first time.

FAMILY LIFE CYCLE

The family life cycle is the process of family formation and dissolution. Using this concept, the marketer combines the family characteristics of age, marital status, and number and ages of children to develop programs and services aimed at various segments.

A five-stage family life cycle with several subcategories has been proposed. The characteristics and needs of people in each life cycle stage often vary considerably. Young singles have relatively few financial burdens, and are recreation oriented. By contrast, young marrieds with young children tend to have low liquid assets, and are more likely to watch television than young singles or young marrieds without children. The empty-nest households in the middle-aged and older categories with no dependent children are more likely to have more disposable income, more time for recreation, self-education, travel, and more than one member in the labor force than their full-nest counterparts with younger children. Similar differences are evident in the other stages of the family life cycle.

Analysis of life cycle stages in market segmentation often gives better results than reliance on single variables such as age. The needs of a twenty-five-year-old bachelor are very different from those of a father of the same age. The family of five headed by parents in their forties is more interested in youth activities than a forty-year-old single person.

FOCUS GROUPS

One of the most popular exploratory research techniques, focus group interviewing, consists of a small group of people (usually eight to twelve) assembled for the purpose of discussing in an unstructured, spontaneous manner topics introduced by a group moderator. The objective of conducting focus groups is *not* to accomplish the goals of a survey at a lower cost. In fact, focus groups, as an exploratory research technique, cannot be substituted for descriptive research survey design. Focus groups are a popular technique and, when appropriately used, they can effectively and efficiently achieve the following goals of exploratory research:

- Generate new ideas or hypotheses, which can be tested in later phases of the research study
- Clarify concepts, actions, or terms used by your target audiences
- Prioritize issues for further investigation
- Provide an opportunity for decision makers to see how their "real" target audience members think, feel, and act
- Obtain an "early read" on changing social trends

Focus groups are good at accomplishing such objectives because their relatively unstructured approach permits a free exchange of ideas, feelings, and experiences to emerge around a series of topics introduced by a moderator. The moderator works from a topic outline that covers the major areas of interest to the client firm, but because each group session consists of different individuals with their own feelings, desires, opinions, etc., no two sessions with the same agenda will be exactly the same in conduct or findings. The term focus group is used because the moderator focuses the group's attention on the predetermined subjects, without letting the discussion go too far afield. However, it is considered unstructured in the sense that a good moderator will consider the particular dynamics of each group when introducing these topics and the order in which they are brought up for discussion.

Focus Group Composition

Conventional wisdom suggests that focus groups should consist of eight to twelve people selected to be homogeneous along some characteristic important to the researcher. Usually, recruitment of focus group participants strives to find people who fit the desired profile but who do not know one another—thus reducing the inhibitions of group members to describe their actual feelings or behaviors. Typically, group sessions last from one-and-a-half to two hours.

Selection and Recruitment of Group Participants

The research objectives and research design will indicate the types of people to be recruited for a focus group. If a facility especially designed for focus group use is contracted with, the management of the facility typically will conduct recruitment of focus group members. If a marketing research firm is being hired to conduct the groups, the firm usually hires the facility; identifies, recruits, and selects the participants; moderates the groups; and makes an oral and written report of the findings. Sometimes the client organization will provide a list of possible participants taken from a master list of members, donors, etc. *At least* four names for every respondent are needed (i.e., approximately fifty names per focus group). Prospective participants are screened when contacted to ensure their eligibility for the group, but without revealing the factors used to assess their eligibility.

Moderator Role and Responsibilities

The moderator plays a key role in obtaining maximum value from conducting focus groups. He or she helps design the study guide, assists the manager/researcher who is seeking the information, and leads the discussion in a skillful way to address the study's objectives while stimulating and probing group participants to contribute to the discussion.

Reporting the Results of Focus Groups

In writing the findings of focus groups, care must be taken not to imply that results typify the target population. The groups were not formed in an effort to generate inferential statistics, but rather to clarify concepts, generate ideas and insights, make the abstract real, etc. Therefore, qualitative rather then quantitative conclusions should be the focus of the written report.

SUGGESTED READING

Krueger, Richard A., *Focus Groups* (Newbury Park, CA: Sage Publications), 1990.
Goldman, Alfred E. and Susan Schwartz McDonald, *The Group Depth Interview* (Englewood Cliffs, NJ: Prentice Hall), 1987.

FUND-RAISING

One of the most obvious and significant differences in the use of marketing by religious organizations compared to for-profit, or even most other not-for-profit, organizations is found in the means by which financial resources are attracted. Figure 4 identifies the sources of funds provided by individuals or organizations in exchange for a church's "products"—either in the form of goods or services, or for intangible social for psychological benefits.

Whatever means of attracting financial resources are selected, maintain a MARKETING ORIENTATION and think of the interaction with the other party as an EXCHANGE process.

Religious organizations are gradually shifting from a product or a sale to a marketing orientation. A marketing orientation calls for carefully segmenting donor markets, measuring their giving potential, and assigning responsibility and resources to cultivate each market. Fund-raisers for religious organizations need to assume that the

Revenue Sources for Congregations

	Individuals	Organizations
Goods or Services	Dinners Publications Rental Property Plays or Concepts Arts and Crafts Education	Denominational Subsidies
Intangible Social or Psychological Benefits	Tithe Pledges/ Commitments Offerings Membership "Dues" Annuities Trusts Life Insurance Benefits	Grants Donations for Specific Causes

*(Left side label: **Religious Organization "Products"**)*

FIGURE 4. Source of Funds Exchanged for a Church's Products

act of giving is really an exchange process in which the giver gets something that the organization can offer in return for his or her contribution.

The first step in the fund-raising process is to study the characteristics of each of the five major donor markets:

1. the congregation as a whole,
2. individuals,
3. foundations,
4. corporations, and
5. government.

Each donor market has its own giving motives and giving criteria.

The second step is to organize the fund-raising operation in a way that it covers the different donor markets, matches potential donors with ministries, and selects the appropriate marketing tools.

The third step is to develop sound goals and strategies to guide the fund-raising effort. Goals are set on either an incremental basis, a need basis, or an opportunity basis.

The fourth step is to develop a mix of fund-raising approaches for the various donor groups. Different methods and material are called for when approaching different groups, such as the mass anonymous small gift market, and the wealthy donors market.

The fifth step is to conduct regular evaluations of fund-raising results.

SUGGESTED READING

Shawchuck, Norman, Philip Kotler, Bruce Wrenn, and Gustave Rath, *Marketing for Congregations* (Nashville, TN: Abingdon Press), 1992, Chapter 11.

GEODEMOGRAPHICS

Marketers segment markets (*see* MARKET SEGMENTATION) in order to be more effective and efficient in finding and communicating with those groups of people with whom the marketer has the greatest chance of engaging in mutually beneficial EXCHANGE. The segmentation "base" refers to the particular variable or set of variables used to divide the market into groups that are homogeneous within the group, and heterogeneous between groups (e.g., if "age" were the segmentation base we might identify four segments: <18, 18-25, 26-50, 51+ years old). Geodemographics is a segmentation base that reflects the "lifestyles" of the U.S. population. Although geodemographics is the generic term used to describe this base, several companies operate proprietary geodemographic segmentation services. Claritas' PRIZM is perhaps the best known of the geodemographic segmentation systems that divide the U.S. population into specific lifestyle segments. All of these systems begin with U.S. Census data and then add other databases to develop detailed descriptions of consumer segments. The PRIZM system divides the U.S. adult population into sixty-two separate lifestyle segments or "clusters" and ranks these clusters in socioeconomic order, giving them snappy names that reflect their ranking, such as "Blue Blood Estates," "Kids and Cul-de-Sacs," "Bohemian Mix," and "Shotguns and Pickups." Each residential address in the United States is classified into one of the segments based upon what the Census data and other databases indicate as the socio-economic, housing, and aggregated consumer-demand information for that household. A "Young Literati" household in Portland, Maine, is more similar in the lifestyle of its members to a "Young Literati" household in Portland, Oregon, than it is to a "Shotguns and Pickups" household located two miles away in the same city. Marketers can identify segments they wish to target and then get a map that shows the geographic areas where those segments are in highest concentration or they can identify specific geographic areas where they desire to penetrate and get a profile of the segments located in that area. For example, PRIZM identifies the following segments present in the zip code 90210, Beverly Hills, California.

PRIZM Rank	Name
1	Blue Blood Estates
2	Winner's Circle
7	Money + Brains
10	Bohemian Mix

The "Blue Blood Estates" are described as:

Elite, Wealthy families
Age group: 45-64
Professionally employed
1.2 percent of U.S. households belong to this segment
They are likely to:
- Belong to a health club
- Visit Eastern Europe
- Buy classical music
- Watch *Wall $treet Week with Fortune*
- Read *Architectural Digest*

This is merely a sampling of the detailed information available for the segments.

Geodemographic segmentation has been successfully used by a large number of religious organizations seeking to identify and better understand those groups of people they wish to engage in exchange processes. For a detailed description of how one denomination has used this approach to better understanding and reaching a target audience see Shawchuck et al. (1992, pp. 184-196). One organization exclusively dedicated to serving religious organizations with demographic and geodemographic data is Percept (see www.percept1.com/pacific/HOMEfront.asp).

REFERENCE

Shawchuck, Norman, Philip Kotler, Bruce Wrenn, and Gustave Rath, *Marketing for Congregations* (Nashville, TN: Abingdon Press), 1992.

SUGGESTED READING

Weiss, Michael J. *The Cultured World: How We Live What We Live, What We Buy, and What It All Means About Who We Are* (Boston: Little Brown), 2000.

GIVING MOTIVATIONS

Why does an individual give to the church or ministry? This is a difficult question to answer objectively, for it is not easy to "know thyself," yet the ultimate worth of any giving is to be found in the motive behind the gift. It would seem that the measure of a person is not so much in what he or she intends or says, but rather in what he or she does.

The motives of giving include the following: obligation and fear, legal compulsion, personal glorification and profit, self-interest, a missionary need, and love. Of these reasons for giving to religion, one of the older reasons and one of interest is obligation and fear of those who give to try to appease their conscience and ensure their salvation. Believing their gifts would help bring salvation to them and their families, landowners in the Middle Ages would endow the Church with property and other wealth. Legal compulsion was also prominent in the Middle Ages, when the Church had governmental power and could require citizens of a community to support the local church.

Although personal glorification, prestige, and honor are often the motives behind the gifts, some givers enjoy the distinctiveness of being paid special attention by the church leaders for the capacity to give large gifts. Gifts given for self-interest reasons have the same intrinsic motives.

Motivation is not easy to define. Someone once said that every person has two reasons for what he or she does—a good reason and a real reason. In other words, there are two separate motives for giving; one is external, or how others will view you for giving or not giving, and the other is internal: you give or do not give due to the credibility of the work needing funds.

People will give to worthwhile causes if they are informed and motivated to give. This usually means they need to know that their gift, even a small one, can be used, and they need to be told how it will be used. Most givers also want a simple "thank-you" from the organizations they support. This assures them that their gift was received and appreciated.

GRID ANALYSIS

A market grid is a two-dimensional view of a market that is divided into various segments based on characteristics of potential constituents. Two important concepts in grid analysis are: first, that characteristics of potential constituents are used to segment the market rather than product characteristics. This ensures a constituent-oriented view of the market rather than a service-oriented view. Second, characteristics of potential constituents rather than existing constituents are used to focus on constituents that the organization may not currently serve.

A series of grids must normally be used to describe a market completely, so the planner must begin with a set of characteristics thought to be useful in differentiating constituents' needs. Each characteristic must be analyzed to determine its probable effect on constituent satisfaction.

Two types of characteristics are useful in the analysis: spiritual and socioeconomic. Some examples of each of these types of characteristics are listed here. Using these characteristics to divide and assign a large group into smaller subgroups enables the planner to isolate the needs of very specific segments and then design programs and services for these segments.

Characteristic Type	Characteristics
Socioeconomic	Age
	Sex
	Income
	Education
	Marital status
Spiritual	Committed/not committed
	Maturity level
	Service orientation

The examples shown are not all-inclusive, of course, but are intended to illustrate the types of characteristics that can be used. A planner must select a specific list of characteristics from the many possible by assessing the impact of a constituent characteristic on need satisfaction. Only those characteristics useful in differentiating needs are used in the market grids. A youth-oriented religious organization might develop a list that includes spiritual maturity, social interaction skills, and degree of peer pressure to segment youth. The spiritual maturity of the youth would certainly influence needs—their ability to understand biblical concepts, ability to verbalize feelings, and desire for spiritual meaning. Once a list of potential constituent characteristics has been developed, the next step is actual grid construction. Each section within the grid is actually a market segment.

IMPLEMENTATION

Implementation puts marketing plans into operation. Marketing implementation involves the daily activities that transform the plan to work. Whereas marketing planning addresses the *what* and *why* of marketing activities, implementation addresses the *who, where, when,* and *how* (Kotler and Armstrong, 2001).

A *Harvard Business Review* article carried the title "Hustle As Strategy" (Bhide, 1986), and the point of the article was that more is gained from a good strategy with great implementation than from a great strategy with good implementation. "Hustle," or implementation, can make or break a company in many marketing situations at the turn of the century. The firm that achieves excellence in the skills needed for implementing a marketing plan may be achieving a competitive advantage that perhaps has eluded it in the strategy development stage of the planning process. However, excellent implementation of a poorly conceived strategy is akin to great advertising of a terrible product—the disaster occurs much sooner than if the excellence was not there! Thus, successful organizations have found ways to be good at both the development and implementation of marketing plans.

Management should place emphasis on developing marketing plans that focus on delivering value to its constituents. From an implementation perspective, the aim is to accomplish this feat by translating the strategy into a series of assigned activities in such a way that everyone can see their job as a set of value-added actions. These actions should be seen as a contribution to the organization by the people assigned to those tasks, because the ultimate result of the actions is greater value being delivered to the customer.

Bonoma (1985) suggested four types of skills that must be utilized in order for such a strategic goal to be successfully translated into implementation activities:

1. *Allocating skills* are used by marketing managers to assign resources (e.g., money, effort, personnel) to the programs, functions, and policies needed to put the strategy into action. For example, allocating funds for special-event marketing programs is an issue that requires managers to exhibit allocating skills.
2. *Monitoring skills* are used by marketing managers who must evaluate the results of marketing activities. These skills can be used to determine the effectiveness of the marketing plan.
3. *Organizing skills* are used by managers to develop the structures and coordination mechanisms needed to put marketing plans to

work. Understanding informal dynamics as well as formal organization structure is needed here.

4. *Interacting skills* are used by marketing managers to achieve goals by influencing the behavior of others. Motivation of people internal as well as external to the company is a necessary prerequisite to fulfilling marketing objectives.

Implementation of the marketing plan includes turning the strategic elements of the marketing mix into tactics. These elements—product, place, promotion, and price—should be viewed from a constituent orientation.

REFERENCES

Bhide, Amar, "Hustle As Strategy," *Harvard Business Review,* September/October, 1986, pp. 59-65.
Bonoma, Thomas V., *The Marketing Edge: Making Strategies Work* (New York, NY: The Free Press), 1985.
Kotler, Philip and Gary Armstrong, *Principles of Marketing,* Ninth Edition (Upper Saddle River, NJ: Prentice Hall), 2001.

INTERNAL MARKETING

Religious organizations, and in fact all organizations, must successfully satisfy the needs of the members of the organization if they are to remain viable and achieve their mission. Satisfying such needs means that the organization successfully manages its EXCHANGEs with members (i.e., it is successful at "internal" marketing). Although such internal marketing can take place in all types of religious organizations, we will illustrate its basic components by describing the process for an individual church congregation.

What Are Satisfied Customers?

What does it mean for a pastor to have "satisfied" church members? It may mean that they are satisfied with the minister's abilities as a preacher, counselor, administrator, enabler, teacher, leader, nurturer, etc. It may mean any of these things or all of them. But it must mean one thing: The members want to continue to remain active participants in the church. Member satisfaction rarely occurs by chance or as a natural consequence of a pastor discharging administrative duties. It would be a mistake to assume that a pastor has more satisfied church members because the *pastor* is better. Members are satisfied because the pastor made *them* better: better at seeking God's presence in their lives, better at relating to their family, better at relating to other members, better at understanding God's plan for them. Pastors should see what they do as "value-added" activities—adding something of value to the lives of their members along some dimension that is significant *from the member's perspective.* This illustrates the need for a shared frame of reference to exist between pastors and parishioners. Pastors must be able to perceive value in church membership from the parishioner's viewpoint so that member satisfaction can be truly delivered by building value into the church.

Several actions taken by a pastor will enhance the likelihood of internal marketing practices leading to having satisfied church members:

1. *The need for visible, personal leadership in instilling a "customer service" mentality in the church.* A pastor must take the lead in building a customer service mentality throughout his or her church. Pastors should make it clear through their own actions that a "Golden Rule" philosophy will prevail in their ministry. Pastors must take the lead in demonstrating that such a philosophy of interpersonal relations will prevail with any interactions between a church officer or staff member and a church member.

2. *Communicating a vision of the church beyond members' previous conception of the organization.* Visionary leadership by a pastor can enable church staff and members alike to envision their church in ways they had not previously seen. This means communicating core values of the organization rather than letting people merely see the church as performing a set of functions.

3. *Understanding what constitutes satisfaction for the target public.* Pastors must focus on understanding their targeted "customers" and being in tune with the needs, attitudes, perceptions, values, and motivations of their members. Pastors should make a point of understanding what it is that their members really value. He or she should develop a "sixth sense" about what constitutes member satisfaction.

4. *Having a clear service strategy instead of assuming that member satisfaction will occur.* Pastors must not assume that just because they enthusiastically support the church's vision that that vision would be put into action whenever a service encounter occurs. Pastors must develop a service strategy for themselves and their church. An effective service strategy is one that noticeably differentiates your church from others, has value in your members' eyes, and is deliverable by the pastor and church staff.

5. *Researching church member attitudes.* Research is no less important when your market is your current church members than it is when seeking new members. Soliciting church members' attitudes not only yields the benefit of knowing where you stand on delivering satisfaction, but its also involves members more actively in the church and its mission. Making members a part of the process of building a responsive religious organization builds "ownership" of the church mission and vision, and has the side benefit of generating new ideas and suggestions, which can result in even greater satisfaction producing activities for the church. A member satisfaction survey which sits unanalyzed and unused is worse than not doing one at all—it generates a lot of unrealized expectations for changed behavior on the part of the pastor and church staff.

6. *Generating commitment throughout the church organization.* Any attempt to dramatically alter the orientation of an organization's members must face the task of turning the "unheard of" into the routine. If a pastor, the church staff, and parishioners are to begin to think in terms of nurturing one another, then they must be routinely talking about the values and ways of making the membership experience satisfying. A pastor must get members of the congregation to think in terms of their roles in serving one another. Routinely talking about the need for and value of nurturing experiences can help staff and members become accustomed to looking for ways to enhance the membership experience. Successful large churches are characterized by being "honeycombed" with groups of laypeople who provide for one anothers' needs and build bonds between members and their church. Pastors should not (cannot) take on a member service/nurturing program alone. Successful service programs require the involvement and commitment of people throughout the organization.

7. *Making sure the basics are well done.* The excellent service organizations never forget that no amount of extras, special touches, or

"fancy packaging" can overcome failure to deliver the core benefits sought from their service by customers. Satisfaction with a church affiliation will not occur unless that experience has enriched the person's spiritual life. Changing the hours of worship to be more convenient, enlarging the parking lot, sending out a church newsletter, etc., will not overcome the limitations of an unfulfilling worship experience. Consider the revealing findings of a 1987 survey in which Lutheran, Catholic, Methodist, and Episcopal Church lay leaders rated their importance of various clergy tasks, then rated their own pastors' effectiveness in those areas. The most striking finding was that 82 percent said

> "deepening parishioners spiritual lives" was "very important" (only preaching ranked higher), but only 33 percent felt that their clergy were "quite effective" at it. This gap has been called "the most important single factor" in the decline of traditional churches. (*Fortune,* 1989, pp. 116-128)

Successful organizations never lose sight of the basics—they know what they have to do and are obsessive about making sure it is done right.

Although it is obviously true that religious organizations should not model all that they do after for-profit business organizations, it is also true that religious organizations cannot defend practices that demonstrate a lack of concern for the welfare of their members. Hence, while a religious organization may not be capable of implementing all the suggestions for internal marketing listed here, it is a rare organization that would not be more true to creating a "Golden Rule" environment by implementing some of these suggestions.

REFERENCE

"Turning Around the Lord's Business," *Fortune,* September 25, 1989, pp. 116-128.

SUGGESTED READING

Albrecht, Karl, *At America's Service* (Homewood, IL: Dow Jones-Irwin), 1988.
Shawchuck, Norman, Philip Kotler, Bruce Wrenn, and Gustave Rath, *Marketing for Congregations* (Nashville, TN: Abingdon Press), 1992, Chapter 10.

LOCATION ANALYSIS

One of the most crucial decisions an organization must make is where to locate. In most instances, this decision cannot be altered for many years, so great care must be exercised in choosing a location. For existing organizations the decision is whether to relocate. This section analyzes this important decision area.

One of the serious risks of any location, no matter how carefully researched and selected, is that conditions may change—making a good location a poor one. Population shifts occur, sometimes rather quickly. Sometimes a big new shopping mall can affect traffic patterns and parking facilities. This means that a long-term perspective must be used in the location decision.

Organizations need to reevaluate existing locations periodically to determine whether conditions have changed or are likely to. If changing locations begins to appear as an alternative, the sooner a new location can be identified, the more time to develop an approach to acquiring the land and/or buildings.

Once the general area has been selected, a major decision facing the organization is the specific place to locate. Even though an area of a city has great potential, if the specific site has inadequate parking or other negative features, then the decision to locate there was a bad one.

The Best Location

Retailers often speak of the "100 percent location"—the best location for the particular kind of store. Churches and ministries can use this same concept. This means trying to identify the best location and then several alternatives that can be pursued if the best location cannot be acquired.

Accessibility of Site by Transportation

With the maze of streets that characterize most cities, we tend to take transportation facilities for granted. Yet there are great differences, and these can attract to or detract from a particular site. In major cities, nearness of public transportation (buses and subways) is important, especially with such constituent groups as the elderly. Traffic congestion and variations during certain periods of the day or week are significant. For example, crowded streets that are made more crowded with factory workers dispersing or with baseball or football crowds can be detrimental to night services or preschool traffic.

The matter of accessibility is rather complex, however. In most larger cities, it is measured in driving time. For example, a location may not be considered if it is over twenty minutes from a major residential area served by a church. This would limit the search for potential sites to those that meet that criterion.

Parking Adequacy

Related to the accessibility of a site is its parking situation. The decline of downtown business is partly due to the scarcity of parking facilities and the expense of such parking. Many large churches have attempted to improve the parking situation by constructing their own garages and ramps, or by arranging for parking at nearby lots. In many downtown areas, it is common to see church signs calling attention to free parking and shuttle service to the church. However, it is difficult to match the parking convenience of the newer suburban locations.

Growth Pattern of the Area

Most locations involve long-term commitments. Therefore, location analysis should consider the direction and growth of the area. Are these improving or going downhill? New stores or buildings and modernization efforts are an encouraging sign. On the other hand, a lack of such updating efforts suggests that present facilities are becoming obsolete, with merchants intending to move to the suburbs as their leases expire. New residential construction and new construction permits should be investigated. For larger cities, projected subway routes can provide a long-term indication of the viability of particular sites.

Compatibility of Existing Organizations

Some organizations are compatible with each other—that is, they benefit from being close together. Others are detrimental. Many cities have specific rules for types of businesses that can be located close to a church or religious organization, but others do not. Nightclubs and liquor stores are examples of businesses not compatible with church or religious organization facilities. Certain things can be detrimental to a particular site and should be evaluated in making a location decision. Vacant buildings create an atmosphere of neglect and poverty. Poor sidewalks, smoke, or unusual noise from nearby factories can be detrimental. Proximity to a bar/nightclub or X-rated movie house flaws a site. If the general area is run-down or poorly lighted, organizations located there probably will suffer. Even a somewhat more intangible factor, the *reputation* of a particular neighborhood for crime or vandalism, will be a negative influence.

MARKET SEGMENTATION

The process of breaking up a market into smaller parts or segments is referred to as market segmentation. The basic premise is that the needs of constituents in one segment are different from those in another, and therefore different marketing strategies should be used to reach different segments. The results of the analysis should be an understanding of constituents' needs by segment and some insight into the types of strategies needed to meet those needs. This is the basis of the entire planning process if a constituent-oriented approach is to be used in planning.

For each segment that is identified, two basic questions must be asked: (1) What are the identifying characteristics of that segment?

and (2) What is its size? Answering the first question helps define constituents' needs and helps develop a profile of constituents for each segment—the qualitative side of the market. The answer to the second question provides information on the size or quantitative side of the market.

Bases for segmentation include geographic, demographic, service usage, benefits sought, and stage in the family life cycle. The most commonly used are geographic and demographic variables.

Geographic segmentation involves use of geographic areas such as county, state, regional, and national as the basis of segmentation. For many religious organizations, this is a logical framework. Many ministries and some large churches concentrate their missionary efforts on only a few counties. They may establish extensive efforts in a few areas and not do anything in others. They are using geographic location to segment the constituents they will serve through missions.

Demographic segmentation uses variables such as sex, age, income, and educational level as the basis for segmenting a market. These variables are appropriate for many types of programs and services—youth, older constituents, etc.

A recent approach to market segmentation concentrates on the usage patterns of constituents. Constituents are classified as users or nonusers, and users are further classified as light, medium, and heavy users. In some situations, a small percentage of the constituents may account for a majority of the users. Preschool programs, counseling services, and home food delivery services for the elderly are examples. Thus, usage rates become important as a basis for segmentation for some programs.

Another way to segment markets is based on the benefits users expect to receive. Constituents may expect spiritual, social, and physical benefits from a certain program or service. Each of these represents the principal benefits sought by the user; and each of these benefit segments, in turn, may be comprised of constituents with different demographic characteristics.

MARKETING

Marketing is the management of an organization's exchanges with its various constituents. A constituent is someone who works for, is a member of, attends, supports, or is affected by an organization. Most people really do not understand marketing and view it as selling, advertising, or public relations. This is readily understandable when you consider the large number of television and radio commercials a person is exposed to every single day. Administrators are often surprised when they discover that selling and advertising are only a part of marketing.

In today's environment, churches and religious organizations must know how to analyze their constituents' needs, attract resources, and use these resources to develop the programs, services, and ideas that will attract and maintain their constituents.

In our definition of marketing, exchange is the central element. Two or more parties enter into an exchange for the mutual benefit of both parties. Each party has something of value to the other, and both parties are better off after the exchange than they were before it took place.

A marketer is someone who has the knowledge and skills to understand, plan, and manage exchanges. The marketer knows how to go about assessing needs of constituents, developing programs to meet these needs, and then effectively communicating what is offered to the constituents.

A more formal definition of church and religious marketing is as follows:

> *Church/religious marketing* is the analysis, planning, and management of voluntary exchanges between a church or religious organization and its constituents for the purpose of satisfying the needs of both parties. It concentrates on the analysis of constituents' needs, developing programs to meet these needs, providing these programs at the right time and place, communicating effectively with constituents, and attracting the resources needed to underwrite the activities of the organization.

Several things need to be emphasized in this definition. First, marketing is grounded in the analysis of the needs of constituents. A marketer does not concentrate on trying to "sell something," but rather identifying and providing for constituents' needs. This need-oriented approach is a fundamental difference between marketing and selling.

Second, marketing concentrates on exchanges that are mutually beneficial for both parties. It does not promote a "win-lose" philosophy but a "win-win" philosophy in which both parties are better off for being involved in the exchange.

Third, marketing's focus is on carefully formulating programs, times, places, communications, and funding activities in relation to the needs of constituents. In this sense, marketing is the response mechanism of the organization. As the needs of constituents change, programs, communication, funding, etc., must change.

Finally, marketing's focus is on the needs of an organization's constituents. The organization does not attempt to meet the needs of everyone, but only those constituents it is best equipped to serve. The doctrinal, denominational, affiliation, if any, and the local environment in which the organization operates ensures that an organization cannot be all things to all people. Marketing helps an organization carefully identify whom it wants to serve. Then the organization's activities are oriented to serve specific constituent groups that are identified through marketing analysis.

MARKETING COMMUNICATIONS

Marketing communication deals with decisions about what is to be communicated, to whom, through what methods and media, and at what appropriate costs. Promotion of programs, services, and activities is necessary to inform, persuade, and remind constituents that a program, service, or activity exists and that constituents can benefit from their participation. For a market to exist, information must be exchanged. Information brings providers and users together at a particular place to engage in an exchange. Communication may be defined as an organization's activities, which are designed to inform, persuade, or remind constituents about the organization and the services it offers.

Insight into the types of decisions involved in communication can be gained by viewing it as a process (see Figure 5). In the communication process, a source (church or religious organization) sends a message by using a certain method or medium. This message is received by a receiver (constituent), and the receiver's words and actions send a message back to the source about what was received and the receiver's willingness to respond to that message. This process is always goal oriented. The sender is communicating to get a response from the receiver. This response may be holding certain information

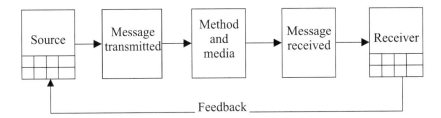

FIGURE 5. The Communication Process

or attitudes, or it may show itself in behavior—immediate acts or precipitant acts—but a response is desired nonetheless.

The checkered areas in the sender's and receiver's boxes represent common frames of reference. A common frame of reference is a prerequisite to effective communication. Unless a common area of understanding is established between the sender and receiver, no communication takes place. The simplest example is a language barrier. If the message is sent in English and the receiver understands only Spanish, no communication takes place. The symbols (words) used to communicate are not common to the two parties in the process.

One point which must always be in the planner's thinking is that promotion from a planning perspective involves sending the right message to the right audience through the right medium by using the right methods at the right costs. Deciding what is "right" constitutes the marketing planner's work in the communications part of the marketing plan.

MARKETING MIX

The marketing mix refers to the elements or variables used to meet the needs of constituents. Marketing orients organizational thinking toward the constituents to be served rather than programs or promotion of existing programs. This is the first step in developing a marketing organization. The second step involves identifying what constitutes marketing variables within an organization. Within a church/ministry setting, these variables are shown in Figure 6.

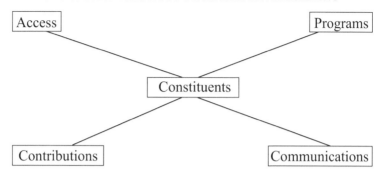

FIGURE 6. Marketing Mix Variables

The needs of the organization's constituents become the focus of the programs offered by the church/ministry. Information about the nature of the organization and the programs offered is then communicated to these constituents. Constituents must have access to these programs at the right time and the right place for their needs to be met. Finally, contributions must be solicited from constituents to support the programs that are offered. Marketing concentrates on meeting the needs of constituents through providing the right programs, with the right communication, at the right time and place, and by generating the right level of contributions from constituents.

All this must be done within the context of the environment in which each church/ministry operates. Each organization has its own unique environment which is created by the community's religious environment, denominational affiliation (if any), community characteristics, and any legal or political pressures which must be addressed by a specific organization. These environments directly affect what the church/ministry can do in altering its programs, communications, etc.; but they are beyond the control of a specific church or ministry. These environmental influences must be considered when evaluating old activities or starting new ones. For example, starting a church day care program would bring local, state, and federal regulations to bear on the organization's activities, because day care centers are regulated by various governmental agencies. Thus, complying with these regulations must be an influencing factor in designing the program.

MARKETING ORIENTATION

Martin Buber's famous I-Thou theological treatise contains the essence of what is meant by applying the concept of marketing orientation to religious organizations. To paraphrase Buber: When we relate to others as *objects* (I-It), we see them in terms of what functions they serve for us. When we relate to them as *subjects* (I-Thou, or I-You), we are conscious that they have feelings about the interaction even as we do. At the risk of oversimplification we summarize the two interactions as follows:

I-It   Using others as tools to help ourselves.
I-You   Using tools to help others.

The I-You relationship is at the heart of a marketing orientation. Nurturing church members via their exchanges with the clergy, other church members, and with external publics is a primary objective of a true marketing orientation. Adherence to a marketing orientation is consistent with the biblical "Golden Rule" of concern for the long-term welfare of others. Marketing-oriented decision makers put themselves "in the shoes" of their exchange partners (e.g., Golden Rule perspective), seeking to understand their needs, motives, perceptions, etc., and then design offerings capable of delivering long-term satisfaction. Authentic marketing-oriented decision makers do not think in terms of "making a sale." Their ambition is to establish such a mutually satisfying relationship that both parties want to continue that relationship on a long-term basis. When translated into a religious organizational setting, a marketing-oriented approach to managing exchanges successfully integrates this service, other-focused perspective, but does not require that the core product of the religious organization be modified to fit market-based desires. A marketing orientation requires the organization to see that the core product—organizational mission, fundamental purpose—can take many tangible forms. The unalterable core should not be confused with the alterable tangible product. For example, many congregations have found creative ways of making worship (the core product) more vital and inspirational to a wider age range of worshipers by making changes in, e.g., the song service (the tangible product). Marketing-oriented leaders of religious organizations are faithful to those ideals deserving of such ardent faith, but are willing to alter those programs of human origin when doing so can better achieve the goal of establishing long-term, satisfying relationships with targeted groups.

Achieving a marketing orientation demands three components to be present:

1. A religious organization must have strong individual marketing orientation among all its key personnel. The organization's marketing orientation is only as strong as the collective sum of the orientation of these people.
2. A religious organization must have its leaders lead by example and reinforce a marketing orientation by the way it adopts an I-You philosophy in all its interactions with employees and members.
3. Leaders who believe in adopting a marketing orientation will formalize that approach to managing exchanges by obtaining measures of success in generating satisfied, loyal members and other exchange partners via surveys, retention data, and other ACTIVE LISTENING methods. (Best, 2000, p. 21)

REFERENCE

Best, Roger J., *Market-Based Management,* Second Edition (Upper Saddle River, NJ: Prentice Hall), 2000.

SUGGESTED READING

Barna, George, *User Friendly Churches* (Ventura, CA: Regal Books), 1991.

MARKETING PLAN

A marketing plan is an operating plan that spells out in detail the results of a situation analysis; a set of objectives to be attained at the end of the year; a detailed tactical statement explaining what must be done, when, and how. In other words, the organizational plan deals with what is to be accomplished in the long run while the marketing plan deals with what is to be done in the marketing area in a given time period, usually a year.

The marketing plan does not necessarily differ in format from the organizational plan. In fact, it must cover some of the same basic topics—objectives, strategies, and so forth. The difference is in scope and time frame. The organizational plan is broad in scope and may lay out a strategy that is never departed from if successful. The marketing plan focuses on the tactical marketing decisions needed to carry out the overall plan. The time frame for the marketing plan is usually a year and normally coincides with the organization's fiscal year. The situation analysis deals only with the current operating environment, and details only important events that influence changes; and the strategy portion contains the detailed tactical decisions that spell out changes in such items as advertising themes, new programs, etc.

The marketing plan is a written document which contains four basic elements:

1. A summary of the situation analysis, including general developments, constituent analysis, and opportunity analysis
2. A set of objectives
3. A detailed strategy statement of how the marketing variables will be combined to achieve those objectives as well as the financial impact
4. A set of procedures for monitoring and controlling the plan through feedback of results

The logic of this approach to planning is clear. We must

1. determine where we are now (situation analysis),
2. decide where we want to go (objectives),
3. decide how we are going to get there (strategy), and
4. decide what feedback we need to let us know if we are keeping on course (monitor and control).

A complete marketing plan provides the answers to these questions.

MARKETING PLANNING

Marketing planning is the process of analyzing an organization's environment, setting objectives, developing marketing strategies, and setting up monitoring and controlling mechanisms.

For marketing administrators, the marketing planning process becomes paramount. The marketing concept or philosophy has no impact on an organization's operating procedures unless it is reflected in the performance of the administrative function of planning. The constituents' needs are the focus of an organization's operations under the marketing philosophy, and this is made evident in the planning process. Which constituent segments will the organization try to serve? How will the marketing functions be performed? Who will perform them? What level of contributions will be achieved? These are all questions that are answered by a well-thought-out and well-written marketing plan. In essence, the plan becomes a tool through which the marketing concept is implemented into the decision-making procedures.

An understanding of the marketing planning process is also an invaluable aid in helping administrators organize their thinking about the marketing process and the various methods and procedures used. When they talk about attendance, administrators relate these items to objectives to be accomplished. A study reporting constituent attitudes toward religious organization activities becomes another aspect of situation analysis. Administrators begin to think systematically and analytically about the marketing process in their organizations, and this in itself may be one of the most crucial contributions of an administrator's involvement in marketing planning.

MARKETING RESEARCH

Research is defined as an organized, formal inquiry into an area to obtain information. When the adjective *marketing* is added to *research,* the context of the area of inquiry is defined. *Marketing research,* then, refers to procedures and techniques involved in the design, data collection, analysis, and presentation of information used in making marketing decisions. More succinctly, marketing research produces the information administrators need to make marketing decisions.

Although many of the procedures used to conduct marketing research can also be used on other types of research, marketing decisions require approaches that fit the decision-making environment to which they are being applied. Marketing research can make its greatest contribution to management when the researcher understands the environment, organization, management goals and styles, and decision processes that give rise to the need for information.

Although the performance of the activities that constitute marketing research requires a variety of research techniques, the focus should be on the decisions to be made and not the techniques used to collect the information. Nothing is more central to understanding the marketing research function and to effectively and efficiently using research in decision making. Any user or provider of marketing research who loses sight of this central focus is likely to end up in one of two awkward and costly positions: (1) failing to collect the information actually needed to make a decision, or (2) collecting information that is not needed in a given decision-making context. The result of the first situation is ineffectiveness—not reaching a desired objective. The result of the second is inefficiency—failing to reach an objective in the least costly manner. The chances of either of these problems occurring are greatly reduced when the decision itself is the focus of the research effort.

To maintain this focal point, one must understand the purpose and role of marketing research in decision making. The basic purpose of marketing research is to reduce uncertainty or error in decision making. The uncertainty of the outcomes surrounding a decision is what makes decision making difficult. If you knew for sure the outcome of choosing one alternative over another, then choosing the right alternative would be simple, given the decision-making criteria. If you knew for sure that alternative A would result in $100,000 in contributions and alternative B would result in $50,000 in contributions, and if the decision criterion was to maximize contributions, then the choice of alternative A would be obvious. However, most decisions must be made under conditions of uncertainty—you do not know for sure if alternative A will produce $50,000 more than B. In fact, it may be that neither alternative is effective. The degree of uncertainty surrounding a decision, the importance of the decision, and the amount of uncertainty that the information will reduce cause information to have value.

Decision making involves choosing among alternative courses of action. It can be viewed as a four-step process that involves

1. identifying a problem or opportunity,
2. defining the problem or opportunity,
3. identifying alternative courses of action, and
4. selecting a specific course of action.

MASS COMMUNICATION MEDIA

Advertising messages must reach constituents through some medium: pamphlets, radio announcements, newspaper ads, etc. Selecting the most appropriate media is an important decision. Although the details of the specific medium used, messages sent, timing, and frequency are usually spelled out in the marketing plan, the planner must also evaluate various alternatives because of the cost involved and the resulting impact on the organization. In many strategies, communications expenditures represent the largest single cost.

Media selection has two broad alternatives—print media and broadcast media. As with many other decisions in marketing, choosing the right mix is what is essential rather than choosing one alternative and not the other.

Even within a category—print, for example—there will usually be a mix of various print media rather than just one type. Media selection begins with the characteristics of the constituents to be reached. Different media have different characteristics, and therefore a matching process must take place. The characteristics of the media used must match the needs of the constituents to which the effort is directed. This is done to maximize reach—the number of different people or households exposed to a particular medium at a given time. For television, the audience varies depending on the time of week, the day, and the specific types of programs offered.

In addition to reach, the frequency and impact of various media must be analyzed. Frequency refers to the number of times an audience is exposed to a particular message in a given time period; impact is the quality of the exposure in a given medium. The importance of additional exposures of the same message or type of message, and the impact of each exposure together with reach, determines media effectiveness; various media costs determine efficiency. The planner is searching for a media combination that is both effective and efficient.

MEASUREMENT

Measurement refers to the process of assessing the characteristics of individuals or organizations from whom we need to collect data. This is a key issue in marketing research projects. The question is "How will we measure what we need to measure?" The answer is one of the most difficult ones facing the researcher. The researcher must often rely on what has been used in past studies and on his or her own judgment to decide upon the appropriate technique.

The researcher must develop operational definitions of the concepts to be measured, and these definitions must be stated explicitly. Even seemingly simple concepts, such as awareness, can be defined in several ways, with each definition having different meaning and relative importance. For 60 percent of the respondents to say they have heard of your church is not the same as 60 percent saying that your church is what comes to mind when they think of a church. Yet both of these approaches measure awareness.

MESSAGE CONTENT

Message content refers to what is said and/or seen in an advertising message or personal contact message. Although the sender is the initiator of the communication process, the process really begins with the receiver—the constituent. This should be obvious, but it is often overlooked in many an organization's desire to tell its "story." Effective communication involves sending the right message, and the right message is the one that will produce the response desired by the organization from the constituent. This is not manipulative, but integrative. The needs and wants of constituents for certain types of information are integrated into the messages that are sent. A simple way to approach this concept is to look at the individual adoption process for new services. This process is made up of the stages a constituent goes through in attending or watching a program, or participating in a service. These stages and the questions a constituent wants answered are shown in the following:

Stage in the Adoption Process	Questions to Be Answered
1. Awareness: Constituent first learns of church/ministry	What are you all about? Who attends/watches you?
2. Interest: Constituent considers whether to try the service	Why would anyone attend? What benefits would they get?
3. Evaluation: Constituent considers whether to try service	Why should I attend or watch? Will I get the same benefits?
4. Trial: Constituent tries service on a limited basis	Will the service really deliver the benefits I expect?
5. Adoption: Constituent decides to attend/watch on a regular basis	Did I make the right choice?
6. Repeat: Constituent will repeat behavior if needs continue to be met	Should I evaluate other services/churches?

As individual constituents move through these adoption stages in larger numbers, the program begins to move through its life cycle—which brings up the need to align the promotion messages with stages in the life cycle. In the introductory stages, communications must inform potential constituents of the offering. In the growth stage, messages must persuade constituents to attend or support a specific service rather than competing services. The maturity stage brings the need for reminding constituents of the services to build repeat attendance. Thus, messages must be developed that answer constituents' questions and reflect the nature of the service at any given time.

Since different constituents will be at various stages of adoption and levels of knowledge and experience, a number of messages conveying different types of information are usually necessary to communicate effectively with different constituents. It should also be emphasized that whereas most constituents are concerned about the benefits received from a service, some constituents are interested in the detailed information that produces the benefits. In attending worship services, for example, many constituents are satisfied to have their questions answered about time and place of the services. However, some may want to know who will speak or sing and what type of presentation will be given—sermon, drama, etc.

The information from the constituent analysis is vital in communication decisions on message content. The needs and motives of consumers become the center of content decisions. Information from testing, where alternate messages are evaluated, and other research to test the message content and probable constituent responses are extremely valuable. If time and money permit, messages should be tested before use, and response measures indicative of constituent responses should be evaluated in the decision-making process.

MINISTRIES PORTFOLIO

Proposed guidelines for identifying the optimal product mix for nonprofit organizations must be altered for religious organizations. Religious organizations such as churches do not typically consider a product's resource attraction potential when considering what products to include in the product mix. Likewise, although some consideration for "market needs" is given to products offered for consumption by external publics, religious organizations do not operate in accordance with the market driven approach (i.e., using customers' needs to determine what we will offer) to product line addition and deletion decisions. Thus, religious marketers require a different set of dimensions to use in developing their product portfolios.

Religious organizations do not use evaluative criteria based on a product's ability to cover its costs, be competitive, or ostensibly enter an attractive market as guidelines for establishing a product mix. Rather, the inclusion of a product in the religious organization's product mix is based upon its ability to fulfill some component of the organization's mission and/or elicit an escalating level of commitment from those internal or external to the organization. In this case, a "balanced portfolio" is one that would include products consistent with these mission goals. The challenge to a religious marketer then becomes one of gaining acceptance of the products consistent with the mission.

MISSION-BASED PRODUCT MIX

Church management theorists generally agree that a religious organization's mission statement should reflect both "vertical and horizontal relationships" and consideration of goals regarding those within and external to the organization with whom the organization wishes to engage in an exchange. Consequently, we can establish two dimensions for a religious organization's mission and two publics, which would be the objects for implementing that mission. This suggests the four-cell matrix as illustrated in Figure 7.

The "core product of mission" dimension consists of the vertical (faith in God) and horizontal (fraternity) mission components. These core comments would be directed at publics internal and external to the organization. The four cells represent the product mix, with the individual cells indicating the product lines within the portfolio. The exaltation and discipleship product line would consist of those activities, such as worship services, prayer meetings, Sunday or Sabbath school classes, etc., which are intended to give praise and prepare members for service to God. The evangelism product line involves those overt religious programs intended to change the thoughts of those external to the organization and to attract new members (evangelism campaigns, literature distributed, radio or TV programs, etc.). The koinonia (Greek word meaning a fellowship of believers) prod-

Targeted Public
of Mission Component

		Internal	External
Core Product of Mission	Faith (Vertical Relationships)	Exaltation and Discipleship (Worship Services)	Evangelism (Overt Religious Outreach Activities)
	Fraternity (Horizontal Relationships)	Koinonia (Fellowship Ministries)	Social Action (Serving Material and Social Needs of Community)

FIGURE 7. Ministries Portfolio Table for Religious Organizations

uct line would include the ministries, services, programs, or offerings of the organization intended to foster a sense of fellowship and community among current church members. The social action product line would include those ministries aimed at helping meet the physical and social needs of those outside the organization's membership. An example of a product mix for these four product lines can be seen in Table 3. The church illustrated in this table is the Willow Creek Community Church of Barrington, Illinois, one of the largest congregations in the United States.

SUGGESTED READING

Lovelock, Christopher H. and Charles B. Weinberg, *Public and Nonprofit Marketing* (Redwood, CA: The Scientific Press), 1989, Chapter 9.

MOMENTS OF TRUTH

A religious organization faces hundreds, if not thousands of moments of truth each day. A moment of truth is any encounter between the organization and a member of one of its publics where the individual gets an impression of the organization.

A moment of truth can be a phone call to the church to ask a question or get someone's address, the response a member gets when making a request for special prayer for a family member in a Sunday school class, the reaction of other members to a dish brought to a church potluck, looking in the pastor's eyes and shaking his or her hand at the end of a worship service, hearing (or not hearing) "thank you for a job well-done" when serving on a church committee, etc. Although a religious organization may not have as many moments of truth as some service organizations such as an airline has each day, it is safe to say that the religious organization's moments of truths are no less important in their contribution to organizational success, and must be managed toward a positive outcome.

A moment of truth does not even have to involve human contact. One of the authors had a conversation with a friend who moved to a new town and sought out the local church on Wednesday night for midweek prayer services. Upon arriving at the unlit church parking

TABLE 3. Willow Creek Community Church Product Portfolio

Mission Objectives (Ministries by Age Group)	Exaltation Product Line:	Koinonia Product Line:	Evangelism Product Line:	Social Action Product Line:
All Ages	Saturday night service Sunday 9 am, 11 am service **Seeds Tapes** of weekend services	Saturday night service Sunday, 9 am, 11 am service **Seeds Tapes** of weekend services	Saturday night service Sunday 9 am, 11 am service **Seeds Tapes** of weekend services Verbal witnessing by laymembers	**Heartbeat**—hospital visitation **Food pantry**—emergency food and clothing for families in need **Hearthstone**—Homebound visitation
Children	**Promiseland**—nursing care and creative playtime for toddler during adult service	**Promiseland**—birth thru sixth grade Bible classes, other activities		**Rainbows**—children suffering from parental loss
Youth	**Camp Paradise**—250-acre camp in Michigan	**SonLight Express**—junior high Saturday AM social activities, spiritual study **Son City**—high school, Thursday evenings social activities and spiritual study **Camp Paradise**—250-acre camp in Michigan	**Son Village**—high school Bible study classes	Premarital Counseling **Alateen**—children in alcoholic families
Single Adults and Couples	**PrimeTime Community** Core Events—Bible teaching, singing, worship **4 Weeks in Focus** Bible study small groups **Odyssey** (singles mid 40s+) social and spiritual events **Grasp**—single-parent families Women's Ministries	**PrimeTime Community** Nights (age 18-30) All-community nights (ages 30-mid 40s) **Odyssey** (singles mid 40s+) social and spiritual events **Grasp**—single-parent families **Voyagers**—(couples in mid 40s+) social and spiritual events	**Outreach** Events (ages 18-30) **All-Focus** Events (ages 30-mid 40s) Small groups	**Child**—pregnant single women **Rebuilders**—marriage breakdowns **Good Sense**—budget counseling **HEAL**—sexual addiction counseling **Heritage**—nursing home visitation **Exodus**—families of people in prison

Source: Adapted from Willow Creek Church printed material.
Note: Programs in bold print are "brand name" ministries of Willow Creek Community Church, Barrington, IL.

lot she saw light coming from an upstairs window, where she expected to find the service being held. Trying several locked doors without success she returned home without making contact with the worshippers. She also reported that the following weekend she tried another local church of the same denomination, was made to feel most welcomed and appreciated, and eventually made the second church her new "home." If moments of truth are not successfully managed, then the quality of the experience for the individual regresses to mediocrity. This impression of mediocrity may then be transferred to other, inexperienced aspects of the organization ("If the main worship service is unfulfilling, I can imagine what the Sunday night service might be like."). But this works both ways—a well-managed and positive moment of truth can provide a "halo" for the organization as well. Of course the administration cannot be present at each moment of truth to manage its occurrence. Therefore, all personnel should receive "customer service training" so that they see themselves as contributing to positive moments of truth for the church. The organization's employees, officers, or members then become the managers of their moments of truth when encountering someone who will form an impression of the institution and its people. Likewise, because the moments of truth may sometimes not involve a person-to-person contact, the systems and "hardware" of each moment of truth occasion must be devised in such a way as to leave a positive impression. For example, what does a church's listing in the yellow pages suggest in the eyes of someone seeing it for the first time? What impression would someone have of a church when driving by? What is the impression left by the moment of truth when someone hears the recorded message on the telephone answering machine at the church office? In all of these and similar moments of truth we must be capable of seeing things through the eyes of the beholder rather than our own.

When considering how to mange the moments of truth, see them as events or specific occurrences rather than as traits. That is, the trait of courtesy for greeters at the entrance for worship service is not the same as a moment of truth for me when I come to your church. If the greeters are generally courteous but are just having a bad day when I arrive, a failed moment of truth will occur. A moment of truth is an episode—a specific event in time—in which someone will encounter the organization in some way and form an impression based on that encounter. It means the difference between being satisfied that you are "generally" leaving the impression you desire and being concerned that each moment of truth will, as far as you can manage it, turn out positive. It might not be too great an exaggeration to say that getting organization members to see their role in the organization in terms of managing their moments of truth to be positive events could become the single most significant step in improving your "customer service."

SUGGESTED READING

Carlzon, Jan, *Moments of Truth* (Cambridge, MA: Ballinger), 1987.

NEW PROGRAM DEVELOPMENT

New program development is the process of adding new services or programs to an organization's existing programs. Developing successful new programs is the key to continued progress for most organizations and a key way to avoid decline.

Most programs reach a point of saturation, and without new programs or changes in existing programs, they tend to decline over time. Research into program failures and successes and the experiences of many marketing administrators have led to the idea that development of a new program or service should be viewed as a series of stages. The completion of one stage leads to a decision of "go" or "no go" concerning the next stage. Each additional stage undertaken represents more investment in time and money, and it should not be taken unless the outcome of the previous stage has been positive. At any stage, a program or service that fails to measure up to predetermined standards is dropped or altered before moving to the next stage. The six stages in new program development are the following:

1. Idea generation
2. Feasibility analysis
3. Program development
4. Constituent tests
5. Test offering
6. Full-scale program offering

If the marketing plan calls for new programs or services, these developmental stages should be followed in the order specified when possible.

Idea Generation

Ideas for new programs and services come from many sources. Constituents, other ministries, seminars, and Christian literature are some of the most common. Some organizations consciously set out to create new ideas, whereas others do not. It usually depends on the perceived importance of new program ideas to an organization's success and the imaginativeness of the administrators. Ideas for new programs must be evaluated by comparing the program or service with constituent needs and resources. This analysis should end with the decision to proceed to the next step, drop the idea, or gather more information.

Feasibility Analysis

If the program or service passes the idea stage, the next stage is a feasibility analysis. Feasibility analysis involves answering a series of questions about the new program:

1. What are the anticipated benefits of this program to constituents?
2. How many people are likely to participate?
3. What costs (dollars, time, or effort) are associated with the program?
4. Are resources needed more desperately in another area?

Answering these questions provides a preliminary assessment of the viability of the program.

Program Development

Given that the questions about the program or service are answered favorably in the feasibility analysis, the next stage is actual program development. The objective of this stage is to develop the program or service to determine if there are any insurmountable problems and to generate detailed descriptions of the program for further testing. For example, what specific skills are needed to carry out the program? Who within the church/ministry possesses these skills? Detailed descriptions of the who, what, when, where, why, and how of the program will result in a detailed outline of the potential program that can be evaluated by others.

Constituent Tests

If the developmental process proceeds to this point, we are ready to bring in constituents in a direct way. Constituent testing can range from a trial program to a roundtable discussion with constituents who are likely to support the program. These tests are especially beneficial because the program can be evaluated by the constituents who will participate in it. This can lead to discovery of both positive and negative elements of the program before it is introduced to an entire group.

Results of these tests may lead to ideas for other new programs, or may necessitate substantial changes to overcome constituent resistance. Remember, it is much easier to correct problems at this stage than after the program is implemented. The rush to get a program started can cost a church dearly when the program fails to live up to expectations. Some ideas take years to develop into successful programs.

Test Offering

After completion of the constituent tests and any alterations in programs or services, the next stage is test offering. In a test offering, the program or service is offered on a limited basis, in a form as close as possible to the final one. This stage offers an answer to a question vital to a program's success: Will constituents participate in the offering in sufficient numbers to justify full-scale program development? This can be considered the acid test for new programs. No matter how well conceived or designed, the final choice is with the constituents. Their votes in participation are the determining factor of success. Unless it is impossible to test offer the program or service, this stage should not be omitted regardless of how promising the earlier stages have been. Again, the organization has an opportunity to get "up on the learning curve" for the program or service. Given the high failure rate of new programs, it is critical that information from a test offering be available for adjusting the program to increase the chances of success.

In addition to a more realistic estimate of participation by test offerings, alternate programs can be tested to determine their impact. For example, alternate locations can aid in estimating constituent sensitivity to location. Such information is invaluable in determining the best location.

Full-Scale Program Offering

Once the program or service reaches this stage, substantial investment has already been made, but the chances for success have been substantially increased. The marketing tasks, however, are still substantial. The decisions at this stage hinge on when to introduce the program or service, and with what specific strategy. The answers to these questions depend on the seasonality of the program, resources, and policies, and results of the test offerings.

NICHE MARKETING

Niche marketing is the selection of a single marketing segment and the development of strategies to uniquely address the wants and needs of the selected single segment. A marketing mix is developed to appeal exclusively to that one part of the market. This practice is also referred to as concentrated marketing.

Why would an organization choose one segment only? This approach is often used by smaller organizations that lack the resources of competitors. For example, a small church could concentrate its efforts on building an outstanding youth program and appeal to families with kids under eighteen years of age. Another reason for the use of niche marketing is that the church leadership may believe that it has a competitive advantage in meeting the needs of the selected segment. If the church considers its location as a strong competitive advantage, it may develop a marketing mix to appeal to the people who live near the church.

An advantage to serving a niche market is that it narrows and clarifies the focus of the marketing organization. It could be viewed as following the KISS principle—Keep It Simple Stupid. If an organization develops a specific expertise, it can be extremely good at serving the wants and needs of the single market.

The danger of selecting and serving one segment of the market is that all of the organization's hopes rest with that one segment. If the segment is too small, shrinking, not easily accessible, or if competition can successfully target the niche, severe problems could result. Therefore, care should be used in selecting the segment.

In addition to niche marketing, a marketer has two other targeting strategies available. One option is undifferentiated marketing. This mass marketing approach treats all customers with the same marketing mix. It uses the same appeals to a broad range of customers, and can be beneficial if the wants, needs, and perceptions of all the people are the same. The advantages of using this method are that cost savings are possible in both the marketing and the development of programs.

Undifferentiated marketing offers one product/service for everyone. The risk of this option is that competitors may develop specialized programs that may better satisfy some segments of the market.

The last targeting strategy available is differentiated marketing. This strategy selects several segments of the market to target and develops different marketing mixes for each segment. If programs are designed specifically for each group, a church can provide a higher level of satisfaction for each individual segment than would have been provided under an undifferentiated approach. In addition, the church can positively appeal to more people than under the niche approach.

The downside of the differentiated marketing strategy is that it increases costs. More programs are involved, and more administration and organization are required.

OBJECTIVE AREAS

Marketing plans for churches/ministries usually contain three types of objectives—attendance (viewing), contributions, and constituents. Short-term objectives are stated for the operating period only, normally one year, whereas long-term objectives usually span five to twenty years. Examples of both types will be given in this section.

Attendance

Attendance objectives relate to an organization's impact on an area, and are a basic measure of the level of activity for a program or service. Attendance objectives are closely tied to scheduling of services, budgeting, and so on.

Attendance objectives may be stated numerically or as a percent of the total number. If the objectives are stated in percents, they also need to be converted to numbers for budgeting and estimating the audience size. Examples of attendance objectives can include

1. Achieve average attendance of 500 for Sunday school by (date).
2. Have 50 percent of the potential TV audience view our annual Christmas special by (date).

The way objectives are stated must reflect what the organization can realistically expect to attain under a given plan. Also, the steps of setting objectives and developing strategy in preparing a marketing plan should be viewed as interactive. In setting objectives, they are first stated in terms of what we want to accomplish, but as we develop the strategy we may discover that we cannot afford what we want. The available resources committed to a given program or service may not be sufficient to achieve a stated objective; if the planning process is resource controlled, the objectives must be altered. It must be remembered that objectives are not fate, but they are direction. They are not commands, but they become commitments.

Each of the objectives shown as follows is clear, concise, quantifiable, and stated within a given time period. Only one of them, Objective 2, requires external data to evaluate whether it was accomplished. Total audience size would be required to compute the percent.

Contributions

Contributions are a vital part of any church/ministry. Although they are never ends in themselves, they are the enabling resources that are needed by an organization.

However, there is a more practical reason for including a specific statement about contributions: it forces the planner to estimate the resources needed to underwrite specific programs and services. A statement of whether resources will be available cannot be made without at least some analysis of the cost of providing services for activities— which must break even. For new programs, the expenditures and contributions associated with the program should have been analyzed before introduction. For existing programs, contributions can be analyzed to project continued levels of support. This information, combined with estimates of expenses involved in implementing the marketing strategy, provides a basis for statements of objectives about contributions. The following are sample statements of contribution objectives:

1. Produce net contributions of $180,000 by (date).
2. Generate a 20 percent increase in contributions by (date).
3. Produce a dollar contribution of $85,000 for the summer youth camp by (date).

Again, nebulous statements such as "acceptable contribution levels" or "reasonable contributions" should be avoided because of the possible variations in definition and the lack of quantifiablity. The objective of a percentage increase in contributions is the only one requiring additional information for its evaluation. The total previous contribution would be required to determine whether this objective has been reached.

Again, the interactive processes of setting objectives and developing strategies must be used to set objectives that are realistic. The costs of many aspects of strategy cannot be estimated until a written statement of strategy is developed. If the marketing strategy calls for a new brochure, for example, that strategy must be spelled out in detail before production and media costs can be estimated.

Constituents

Constituent objectives may seem unusual to some, but their inclusion should be obvious. They serve as enabling objectives in attendance and contribution, and also represent specific statements of constituent behaviors and/or attitudes an organization would want consumers to have toward its programs and services, as seen in the following sample statements:

1. Create at least 80 percent awareness of the existence and nature of our new recreational center in the ten-to-twenty-two age segment of the market by (date).
2. To have at least 80 percent of our constituents favorably rate our programs in our next survey by (date).

Constituent objectives are especially important in providing direction to the development of the promotional strategy section of the marketing plan. As previously shown, they specify results desired of constituents in terms of behaviors and attitudes, and should have the same characteristics as other objectives. They must be stated in objectively measurable terms and should be evaluated in relation to their accomplishment as a part of the monitoring and control system used in the plan.

OBJECTIVES

Marketing objectives can be defined as clear, concise written statements outlining what is to be accomplished in key areas in a certain time period, in objectively measurable terms that are consistent with overall organizational objectives. Objectives are the results desired upon completion of the planning period. In the absence of objectives, no sense of direction can be attained in decision making. That is, "If you don't know where you are going, any road will get you there."

Marketing, objectives answer one of the basic questions posed in the planning process: Where do we want to go? These objectives become the focal point for strategy decisions.

Another basic purpose served by objectives is in the evaluation of performance. The objectives in the marketing plan become the yardsticks used to evaluate performance. As will be pointed out later, performance cannot be evaluated without some standard with which results can be compared. The objectives become the standards for evaluating performance because they are the statement of results desired by the planner.

Objectives have been called "the neglected area of management" because in many situations there is a failure to set objectives, or the objectives which are set forth are unsound and therefore lose much of their effectiveness. In fact, an approach to management, called management by objectives (MBO), has emphasized the need for setting objectives as a basic managerial process.

One approach to writing marketing objectives that contains these characteristics is to apply a set of criteria to each statement to increase the probability of good objectives. One such list follows:

1. *Relevance.* Are the objectives related to and supportive of the basic purpose of the organization?
2. *Practicality.* Do the objectives take into consideration obvious constraints?
3. *Challenge.* Do the objectives provide a challenge?
4. *Measurability.* Are the objectives capable of some form of quantification, if only on an order of magnitude basis?
5. *Schedule.* Are the objectives so constituted that they can be time phased and monitored at interim points to ensure progress toward their attainment?
6. *Balance.* Do the objectives provide for a proportional emphasis on all activities and keep the strengths and weaknesses of the organization in proper balance?

Objectives that meet such criteria are much more likely to serve their intended purpose. The resulting statements can then serve as the directing force in the development of marketing strategy.

Consider the following examples:

Poor: Our objective is to maximize attendance.
Remarks: How much is "maximum"? The statement is not subject to measurement. What criterion or yardstick will be used to determine if and when actual attendance is equal to the maximum? No deadline is specified.
Better: Our attendance target for worship services in the next calendar year is an average of 1,000 per week.

Poor: Our objective is to increase contributions.
Remarks: How much? A $1 increase will meet that objective but is that really the desired target?
Better: Our objective this calendar year is to increase contributions from $30,000 to $35,000.

Poor: Our objective next year is to boost advertising expenditures by 15 percent.
Remarks: Advertising is an activity, not a result. The advertising objective should be stated in terms of what result the extra advertising is intended to produce.
Better: Our objective is to boost our viewing audience from 8 to 10 percent next year with the help of a 15 percent increase in advertising expenditures.

Poor: Our objective is to be the best church in our area.
Remarks: Not specific enough; what measures of "best" are to be used? Attendance? Contributions? New programs started? Services offered? Number of converts?
Better: We will strive to become the number one church in the metropolitan area in terms of new converts baptized during the next calendar year.

ORGANIZATION AND PROGRAM LIFE CYCLES

Religious organizations, programs, and specific services go through a predictable cycle. The potential of such a cycle points out the need for continually reviewing what an organization offers its constituents in terms of programs and services. These must be evaluated regularly to determine if new programs and services are needed, or if existing ones should be changed.

The organization or program is founded at some point and grows slowly. This is usually followed by a more rapid period of growth if the organization or program is successful. The growth eventually slows down and the organization or program enters maturity. This is followed by a period of decline as long as the organization or program fails to find a new mission. This life cycle model has been used not only to describe organizations and programs, but also the history of services, ministries, and specific activities.

The organization life cycle can be refined for each institutional sector through observing a large number of cases. Dr. John Shope, a church planning consultant, described the theoretical life cycle of a church as falling into eight stages:

1. The church is organized.
2. The nucleus of the church organization survives and grows slowly.
3. The growth rate increases due to the confidence of potential members being translated into church participation and membership.
4. The membership plateaus. Membership in the church stabilizes, and contentment and routine become obvious in the membership and church program.
5. Initial decline—membership of the church declines, little is done to reverse trend.
6. Rapid decline—membership decline accelerates, members find logical excuses to join other churches.
7. Nothing but a small nucleus of members remains, the church is a financial burden to those who stay.
8. Dissolution—the congregation disbands and the church dissolves. (cited in Kotler, 1982, pp. 81-82)

REFERENCE

Kotler, Philip, *Marketing for Nonprofit Organization,* Second Edition (Englewood Cliffs, NJ: Prentice Hall), 1982, pp. 81-82.

ORGANIZATION STRUCTURE

The organizational structure is simply the relationship of activities, authority, and responsibility at a given time within the organization. The nature of the organization greatly influences not only who will be responsible for marketing, but also how much assistance the individual can expect from others in the organization.

Two basic types of marketing organizational structures are the line organization and the staff organization. The distinctions between the two are the separation of planning and operating tasks in the staff and line organization. The line organization is the simplest form and will be described first.

In a line organization, authority flows directly from the chief administrator to the first subordinate, then to the second, and so forth. Few, if any, specialists are present in the organization, and the same individual usually performs planning and operating activities. In fact, the chief administrator may do all the planning for all areas and maintain primary authority and responsibility for all areas.

In the marketing line organization, the marketing administrators are responsible for planning and for the operations in marketing. The two people reporting to the chief marketing administrator are responsible for the activities indicated by their titles. No staff personnel are available to provide support to these marketing administrators. Although this type of organization may be successful for small organizations, its usefulness in larger, more complex situations is limited.

To be effective, there must be a division of effort, and this is exactly what staff positions provide. Staff personnel are added to help the line personnel perform the various functions carried on in an organization, especially the planning function. A marketing administrator in a line organization must not only develop plans but also carry them out. This means there is less time available for planning, because the administrator is involved in operating tasks of the organization. Good planning procedures an be used under these conditions, especially if there are only a few programs and/or constituent groups. However, the analysis done as a part of the planning process usually will not be as thorough, simply because of less time and fewer resources available to the administrator.

The line and staff organization adds staff specialists to the organization to support line positions. This permits separation of planning and operating activities, which in turn means more time and re-sources available for marketing planning. The result should be more thorough plans.

These staff specialists are available to undertake efforts in their ar-eas of specialization. Of course, there are many other ways to special-ize staff personnel—programs, constituent types, and so on. A wide variety of potential organizational structures can be adapted to a spe-cific organization's needs.

PERFORMANCE EVALUATION AND CONTROL

Performance evaluation and control refers to the process used to evaluate the effectiveness of marketing activities. Performance should be evaluated in many areas to provide a complete analysis of what the results are and what caused them. Two key control areas are attendance and promotional activity and contributions and constituents' atti-tudes. Objectives should be established in all of these areas within the plan.

Attendance Control

The attendance control data listed in Table 4 are from an analysis of attendance for individual programs or services. Attendance can be evaluated on a program-by-program basis by developing a perfor-mance report as shown in Table 4. When such a format is used, the at-tendance objectives stated in the plan are broken down on a quarterly basis and become the standard against which actual attendance re-sults are compared. Number and percentage variations are calculated, because in some instances a small percentage can result in a large number variation.

A performance index can be calculated by dividing actual atten-dance by the attendance objective. Index numbers of about 1.00 indi-

TABLE 4. Attendance and Performance Report Quarter 1 (By Program)

Program	Attendance Objective	Actual Attendance	Percent Variation	Variation	Index Performance
A	1,000	900	100	−10.0	.90
B	950	1,020	+70	+7.4	1.07
C	1,200	920	−280	−23.0	.77
D	2,000	2,030	+30	+1.5	1.02

cate that expected and actual performance are about equal. Numbers larger than 1.00 indicate above-expected performance, and numbers below 1.00 reveal below-expected performance. Index numbers are especially useful when a large number of programs are involved, because they enable administrators to identify programs that need immediate attention.

Promotional Activity

Promotional activity is another important area necessitating control. It should include assessment of personal and nonpersonal means of contacting constituents.

Personal Contact Data

A great deal of analysis of performance can be done on personal contact data. These data can be divided into qualitative and quantitative inputs.

Qualitative inputs:	*Quantitative inputs:*
1. Time management	1. Days worked
2. Planning effort	2. Calls per day
3. Quality of presentation	3. Proportion of time spent in contacts
4. Church/ministry knowledge	4. Expenses
5. Personal appearance and health	5. Miles traveled per contact
6. Personality and attitudes	6. Number of new contacts reached

Analysis of these facts will help an administrator evaluate the efficiency of the personal contact effort. For many of these input factors, an average can be computed to serve as a standard for analyzing individual personnel. If the number of contacts per day for one representative is three and the average is six, this case warrants attention. The low calls per day could be caused by a large, sparsely populated territory, or it could be that the person is spending too much time with each constituent. Whatever the problem, management must be alerted to its existence.

Advertising Data

Advertising inputs are difficult to evaluate, but must be dealt with nonetheless. Several factors can be evaluated, which help determine the efficiency of this input

1. Level of advertising
2. Readership/viewing statistics
3. Cost per thousand
4. Number of inquiries stimulated by an ad
5. Number of inquiries that lead to a visit
6. Changes in attendance generated by an ad campaign

These measures help evaluate the results of advertising decisions. Tracking these data over several years can help identify successful appeals, ads, or media. The key to evaluating performance is the setting of objectives that are the standards by which actual performance can be evaluated.

PERSONAL CONTACT

Personal contact refers to the one-on-one encounters between organizational representatives and constituents. Regardless of the emphasis on personal and nonpersonal contact, every organization has someone who is assigned the responsibility for dealing with constituents. These people are the organization's representatives. Personal contact decisions revolve around five key areas:

1. Quality
2. Number
3. Organization
4. Presentation
5. Compensation

Quality

The quality of the representatives refers to the level of education and experience. The first step in determining the quality needed is to examine the task to be performed by the representatives. If they are basically delivering prepared information, a high level of skill is not necessary. On the other hand, when the information is complex, such as gaining support for a new project, a higher-caliber representative is needed. The quality of the representatives is determined basically by the nature of the tasks to be performed and the importance of the individual representative to the organization. The greater his or her importance to the organization's success, the higher the quality needs to be.

Number

The number of representatives needed in a given time period can be determined in two basic ways. One is a "bottom-up" approach and the other a "top-down." The bottom-up approach begins by identifying the number of constituents to be reached, the amount of time to be spent with each, the number of visits to be made to each constituent per time period and, from this information, the number of constituents each representative can handle. This number is divided into the number of constituents to determine the number of representatives. For example, if each representative should spend an average of one hour with each constituent, visit once a month, and average six visits a day, a representative could handle 120 constituents—six calls a day, five days a week, four weeks a month. When the number 120 is divided into the total number of constituents, the number of representatives can be calculated.

The top-down approach begins with the total number of constituents divided into an equal number of territories; it then determines the number of representatives needed to cover these territories. If the total number of constituents was 1,000 and territories were designed with 100 constituents in each territory, then 10 representatives would be needed.

A combined approach would consider both the workloads of the representatives in terms of number and type of visits and other duties and the number of constituents in each area. This approach would relate both *constituents' needs and representatives' ability.*

Organization

Representatives can be organized three ways: by services represented, geographical area, and constituent type. A fourth possibility would be to combine two or more of these approaches. One of the most commonly used organizational structures is based on geographical areas. This approach is best used when the representative is knowledgeable about all aspects of the organization. This person would answer questions about the organization's services.

Where the complexity of an organization's services and programs do not permit organizing by area, service-based organizational structures are used. In this approach, a separate representative is used to represent different services of an organization. For example, a minister may make contact with new converts, whereas the choir director may call on a family with prospective choir members.

When the needs of constituents are completely different, representatives can be organized by constituent type. A common breakdown used is between members and nonmembers. A variation is with key contacts. Certain people, in larger or more complex groups, are designated as key contacts, and representatives are assigned to visit them. Ecumenical councils are typically considered key groups, and a specific representative may be assigned to this group. Another variation of this structure is to divide by donors and nondonors.

Presentation

The information presented to constituents should not be random thoughts about the organization, but should correctly convey the organization to the individual. Much detailed thought should go into the decisions of the messages delivered to constituents. A well-thought-out presentation of information, ideas, and concepts is much more effective in accomplishing the desired results.

Compensation

An organization can compensate its representatives in both financial and nonfinancial ways. Nonfinancial compensation refers to the opportunity to serve and recognition for service. Financial compensation is monetary in nature, and the representatives are on the organization's staff. Two plans are commonly used for financial compensation. One plan is to pay representatives a straight salary. In this instance, the organization is paying for a unit of time—week, month, or whatever. This plan is commonly used when the representative performs a variety of tasks. It provides maximum security, but may not offer much incentive for above-average performance unless it is carefully administered.

By contrast, another plan used to compensate representatives is based on units of accomplishment or performance rather than units of time. This plan is commonly used when the representatives are involved in fund-raising. It provides maximum stimulus but may not provide much security.

PERSONAL CONTACT PROCESS

The personal contact process refers to the sequence of steps or order of activities used in making contacts with constituents. Although there are many different approaches to this process, the following is a commonly used format.

Step 1: Constituent Identification

The purpose of this step is to identify specifically who will be contacted. Information such as spelling and pronunciation of names, as well as correctness of addresses and telephone numbers, should be verified at this stage.

Step 2: Preapproach

This step is used to collect information that would be helpful in relating to constituents. Their prior contact with a church or religious organization, their personal and family background, their religious experiences, church membership, occupation, etc.

Step 3: Approach

This step refers to how to begin the conversation with the constituent. Approaches include: (1) *referral,* "Mrs. Jones said you were interested in . . . "; (2) *reminder,* "You filled out a card requesting a visit . . . "; and (3) *question,* "Would you be interested in hearing how . . . ?"

Step 4: Telling Your Story

The representative tells the story of the church or religious organization. It includes information on what the organization is, what it does, and what benefits the constituent would receive from affiliating with the organization. Many organizations have material printed for the representative to give to the constituent. This provides consistency in what information is provided to constituents. It also provides the representative with something specific to say about the organization.

Step 5: Answering Questions

The communication process must not be one-way. The constituent must be given the opportunity to answer questions and make comments. The questions and comments are feedback that enables the representative to respond to questions the constituent is interested in.

Step 6: Closing Comments

This step allows the representative the opportunity to make closing statements. These statements may set up another visit or elicit some specific action from the constituent such as visiting the service or making a pledge of support.

Step 7: Follow Up

The final step is often overlooked by many representatives. A card, letter, or telephone call can reap great rewards in terms of stressing interest in constituents or just letting them know how much you appreciate their time.

POSITIONING

Positioning is the process of creating an image of a church. A position is the perception people have of a particular church relative to other churches and religious organizations. Generally, a church should attempt to differentiate itself from others.

How does a church want to be viewed? For example, several items to consider are youth activities, friendliness, support of sick, formality of worship, type of music, and charismatic level. A church should determine how it wants to be perceived and should build its programs related to these and many other dimensions to achieve the desired position. The target market strategy and positioning decision provide a basis for the development of the marketing mix.

Marketing research can identify perceptions of market offerings. Positioning maps are sometimes used to locate opportunities in the market. For example, if perceptions are measured on senior adult activities and friendliness, the positioning map shown in Figure 8 may result.

The dots on the map represent specific churches in the community. No church in the area is perceived to have many senior adult activities and perceived to be high in friendliness. Therefore, an opportunity is identified in the market. If other factors (such as demographics) are

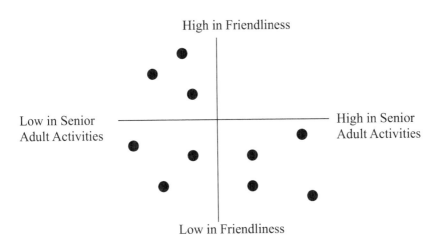

FIGURE 8. Sample Positioning Map

positive, a church could develop its marketing mix to provide an offering that would be perceived to be favorable to senior adults and perceived to be very friendly.

For example, First United Methodist Church of Tulsa, Oklahoma, has always used as a motto, "A Friendly Church Where People Care." This motto is used on church bulletins, the church newspaper, and radio and television promotions. First United Methodist Church is positioning itself as a friendly place where people care about God, one another, and their community.

Another church uses as a motto, "A Place of Worship for All People." Thus one would expect emphasis on worship and openness to all types of people regardless of age, race, sex, or spiritual condition.

When organizations use such phrases or terms to describe themselves and then follow through in activities, emphasis of programs, openness to others, etc., they are reinforcing a basic *position* in the minds of their constituents.

The actions of Rivermont Presbyterian Church in Lynchburg, Virginia, provide an example of positioning. The church leaders—pastors and elders—are united in their theology, and they apply their convictions to their worship and to other programs. Rivermont combines biblical, evangelical preaching with a "blended" worship service that has a traditional liturgical structure and the elements of historic worship (such as the weekly recitation of the Lord's Prayer, the Apostles' Creed, and historic hymns), complemented by the use of a limited amount of contemporary music. Evangelical theology is often associated with less formal worship services that have very casual dress, much contemporary music, and high technology sound and video equipment. Rivermont Presbyterian maintains an evangelical spirit without the contemporary feel.

Rivermont did not explicitly target segments to which this type of worship would appeal. They did not do it for any marketing reason; it is "who they are." Nevertheless, they have established a position in the market by selecting their style of worship services.

PRIMARY DATA

Research conducted to get answers to our research questions, or to test our hypotheses to determine whether or not they are supported by the information we collect, may require us to go beyond the examination of existing data. When we find ourselves in such a situation we are in need of *primary* data—data not available in a secondary form that must be collected to address the specific needs of our research. Research studies can be at any point on a continuum, which at one end answers all research questions with SECONDARY DATA, and at the other end (where) no existing secondary data can be used to answer the research questions.

Types of Primary Data

Primary data come in a variety of forms. Some of the more common types of primary data are discussed here.

Demographic/Socioeconomic Data

Information such as age, education, occupation, martial status, sex, income, ethnic identification, social status, etc., are of interest to marketers because when combined with other types of primary data (e.g., attendance rates, attitudes, etc.), these descriptions help marketers profile target market members or other groups of interest.

Another reason for collecting this information is to test hypotheses that are related to groupings of people by demographic/socioeconomic category (e.g., young people will prefer program A and middle-aged people will prefer program B).

Attitudes

Attitudes refer to a person's feelings, convictions, or beliefs about an object, idea, or individual. Attitudes are a common object of measurement for marketing researchers because it is believed that they are precursors of behavior. (*See* ATTITUDE MEASUREMENT.)

Psychographics/Lifestyle Data

This type of data is concerned with people's personality traits, what interests them, how they live, and their values. It is sometimes referred to as a person's AIOs—activities, interests, and opinions. Marketers find that combining psychographics and lifestyle information with demographics provides a "three-dimensional" perspective of a target market, permitting a much better focus to a marketing program.

Intentions

Intentions refer to the anticipated future behaviors of an individual. This is a subject of interest to marketers who factor the planned behavior of their target audience heavily into marketing plans.

Awareness/Knowledge

Referring to what subjects do or do not know about an object of investigation, awareness, and knowledge is of interest to marketers who wish to distinguish the image, experience, feelings, etc., of subjects who are familiar with a program from those who are not.

Motivations

Motives consist of inner states that direct our behavior toward a goal. Other terms used to describe motives are urges, drives, or impulses. Our concern with motives centers around an interest in why people act as they do. When we ask respondents to indicate how important each of several program attributes is in influencing their choice we are attempting to identify what motives are influencing their behavior.

Behaviors

Behaviors are the actual actions taken by respondents. Obtaining information about a person's behaviors might be accomplished through either self-report, or observation, either disguised or undisguised, of a subject's behavior as it occurs.

Methods of Collecting Primary Data

The main methods of collecting primary data are communication and observation. Communication includes various direct approaches of asking questions of respondents by either personal interview, telephone survey, electronic survey, or mail questionnaire. Observation, on the other hand, involves the process of viewing behavior either in the field or in laboratory settings. In this method of data collection, an observer records activities of the entity being observed, either in a structured (descriptive or casual research) or unstructured (exploratory) fashion. Sometimes mechanical devices are used instead of an observer to record the actions of interest.

SUGGESTED READING

Wrenn, Bruce, Robert Stevens, and David Loudon, *Marketing Research* (Binghamton, NY: The Haworth Press), 2002.

PROGRAM OFFERINGS

Although many churches and ministries may start out by offering only one basic program or set of programs, most develop a line of programs which may not be complementary, or that even compete with each other. One large church that wanted to orient its members to local missions developed over twenty new programs aimed at community missions. Members had to choose which to participate in because they conflicted in days/times offered.

Reasons for developing a line of programs rather than concentrating on just one or two include (1) more people can be involved in leadership positions, and (2) greater community impact.

Two problems must be dealt with in developing a group of programs—cannibalization and diversification into areas beyond the organization's abilities. Cannibalization occurs when a new program or service is added and it takes away from another program already established. In some cases this is unavoidable, but cannibalization must be evaluated in estimating participation in a new program.

The other problem occurs when an organization fails to evaluate its ability to handle a new program. Feeding homeless or less fortunate people is a worthwhile cause, but the volunteers and financial resources must be large enough to launch *and* sustain such a program.

Selecting program names is a related decision. A good program name is not only a necessity for constituent recognition but also a valuable asset. Choosing an appropriate name is an important decision because constituents' satisfaction can be increased, and word-of-mouth advertising can be used to promote the program.

Three basic attributes of a good program name are: easy to pronounce, easy to recognize, and easy to remember. Constituents should be able to pronounce the name in only one way to avoid confusion. The name should also suggest some positive attributes of the program. "Hour of Power," "Praise and Worship," "Joyful Day Preschool," and "Pack the Pew Night" are all suggestive of the attributes of the program or service.

PROGRAM/SERVICE ELEMENTS

Program/service elements deal with the concepts and decisions that must be made about new and existing programs. This includes decisions about their development, determining appropriate attributes, decisions on the number of programs, and various other elements of program management. Administrators face these major decisions when developing programs and services for a church or ministry marketing plan.

Planning of the marketing mix begins with the programs or services to be offered. Contributions, promotional mixes, and access decisions are all related to the "product" or service to be offered to constituents. A marketing view must be taken to understand fully what is meant by the term "program" and to develop programs with the right attributes.

Nowhere is the interaction of marketing, contributions, and personnel more critical than in program decisions. All three areas are directly affected, and input from all of them is a prerequisite to successful program planning.

A few examples will help illustrate the broad meaning that the term "program" can have from a constituent or marketing viewpoint. Robert Schuller's Sunday morning program, aired for many years, is called *The Hour of Power.* What if the nature of the program remained unchanged but the name were changed to *Hour of Weakness*? Would as many people tune in on Sunday? Would the whole program be viewed from a different perspective?

A program is more than just the activities that make it up, and a service is more than just its end results. From a marketing perspective, a program or service may be defined as the sum total of all physiological, psychological, esthetic, and spiritual satisfactions derived from participation in a program or service. This means that a program or service must be conceived from a total perspective, and not from a narrowly defined one of the activities involved. The environment of the program, the name or symbol used, the location and who might attend, are all a part of constituents' perceptions of a program. Not to understand this point can mean not only program failure, but also failure to reinforce several user satisfactions at the same time.

For example, a mother enrolling her child in a church's day care program may be primarily interested in a safe, positive environment. But not to consider the choice of the name of the program is to miss a chance to add symbolic satisfaction to the use of the preschool. A name such as "Joyful Day Preschool" adds a feeling of a happy atmosphere that could be missed with a name such as "First Church Preschool."

For churches and ministries, this is an extremely important concept since most offer many programs. What is a church or ministry? It is really the constituents' perceptions of the whole church or ministry, programs, personnel, layouts, smells, colors, and so on. Again, the total offering must be considered, not just the narrow view of a program in a purely physical or spiritual context.

PROMOTION BUDGET

An organization must determine the amount of funds it should spend on promotion. Ideally, a marginal analysis would be used when budgeting; that is, more dollars should be spent on promotion as long as benefits exceed the costs. However, the benefits of promotion are often delayed and difficult to measure. Also, the reality of most organizations is that they want to spend more on promotions than they have the capacity to spend. Therefore, a method should be developed to determine the level of spending.

The percentage of revenues method is popular. This is developed by taking a certain percentage of last year's revenues or this year's expected revenues. The advantage of this method is that it is simple and, if based on reliable past information and a stable environment, it can work well. The disadvantage is that this method may not consider the objectives and strategies of the church; if these factors or the revenues are changing, this method may not be appropriate. If, for example, revenues are declining for whatever reason, this method may not provide the needed funding for special church promotions that may be deemed to be necessary.

Another way of determining the promotion budget is called the match competitor method; a church would spend about the same amount of dollars as other churches in their community. This system helps a church "keep up" with its competition, but the downside is that it may produce a budget that is not in accordance with its vision. Again, each church has its own objectives, needs, and strategies which demand a particular level of promotion.

Many churches use an available funds method, in which they will spend as much as they can afford. The advantage is that this system controls expenses. The problem is that it does not recognize and gain the possible benefits of promotion and marketing.

The objective-task method establishes promotion objectives and then determines the costs to achieve the objectives. This rational approach is businesslike and can work well when a particular campaign can be easily measured. However, this method is difficult to implement and is based on estimates.

Other methods that can be used are share of market, share of voice, empirical research, amount per member, and quantitative mathematical models. These generally are not appropriate for churches and are not discussed here.

Once the promotion budget is established, the church then can divide the funding into each area—advertising, public relations, personal selling, and church promotions. The church management should establish specific objectives for each area and should evaluate each for costs and benefits.

PROMOTIONAL MIX

The promotional mix is the combination of the communication elements—advertising, personal selling, public relations, and church promotions—that an organization selects to achieve its promotional objectives. These elements should be integrated and coordinated with the marketing mix. The diagram in Figure 9 depicts the marketing mix and the promotional mix.

FIGURE 9. Marketing Mix and Promotional Mix Diagram

Each of the promotional mix components has advantages and disadvantages (see Table 5). A church should choose an optimal blend of these variables based on its theology, goals, resources, personnel, abilities, and promotion budget.

PUBLICITY

Publicity refers to communications about an organization that appear in or are heard about in nonpaid space or airtime. Publicity, when properly managed, offers another opportunity to promote an organization's services, but in a way unlike those discussed thus far. Publicity involves mass communication transmitted through the media in editorial space rather than paid space. Any time an organization or its services creates news through the media, the organization is using publicity. Publicity has been called "the velvet hammer" of communications because it can drive home a point in a different manner.

A church or religious organization having a well-known personality as a guest, starting a new program, or moving to a new location are examples of events that are usually newsworthy to the community or

TABLE 5. Advantages and Disadvantages of Promotional Mix Elements

Promotional Mix Elements	Definition	Examples	Advantages	Disadvantages
Advertising	A paid communication from an identified sponsor using a non-personal medium	Television Billboards Signs Yellow pages Direct mail Radio	Can reach a large group Has control of message, timing, and location	Can be expensive Is often ignored
Personal Selling	Personal communication between an organization's representative and a prospect in an effort to influence the prospect's decisions and behavior to the mutual benefit of both parties	Door-to-door visitation Neighborhood Bible studies Evangelism teams Pastor's calls in response to first-time visitors	Can tailor message to prospect Can get immediate feedback	Has high cost in dollar and time per contact Is dependent upon ability of person representing church
Public Relations	An organizations communications with its publics in an effort to develop good relationships	News articles Newsletters Feature stories Editorial interviews	Creates credibility and positive attitudes toward the organization Is low in cost	Is not in the complete control of the sponsor Is difficult to measure results
Church Promotions	Activities designed to encourage an immediate prospect commitment in a specific time period	Mission trips Picnics Music recitals Marriage enrichment conferences Summer youth conferences	Builds enthusiasm and excitement Produces immediate response	Is short-term Is difficult to differentiate

media audience. When properly publicized, many people can be informed about the organization through the media, and the time or space does not cost anything.

Publicity can also be negative, since mistakes, fires, thefts, failures, and so on also make the news. Publicity should be managed as a part of the organization's communication efforts. Publicity offers a way to impact constituents in new and meaningful ways. Even small churches (less than 100 members), can get involved in big projects to help others and motivate others to get involved too. One such church's efforts were able to motivate local businesspeople to give an estimated $25,000 in equipment and transportation to replace an orphanage's water supply system in a Mexican village.

When the orphanage director brought some of the Mexican children to visit their American friends, one church member decided this could be a publicity opportunity to let other people in the community know about the needs of the orphanage and the work in Mexico. The resulting media coverage involved two television stations visiting the church and touring with the orphans, coverage on a morning talk show, plus radio and newspaper coverage. This publicity brought another outpouring of interest with many calls and letters from individuals, civic groups, and businesses who wanted to help the orphanage.

In one year more was donated to the orphanage in money, supplies, clothing, etc., than in the previous three years combined. In addition, the church received more publicity than any other church in the area. The pastor says people he does not know continue to greet him and ask him about the orphanage *and* his church. His comment about the media coverage was an apt summary of the role of publicity: "We had a story to tell and we simply told our story."

QUESTIONNAIRE

A questionnaire is the main type of data-gathering instrument in DESCRIPTIVE RESEARCH designs. A questionnaire is a set of questions for obtaining useful information from individuals. Since poor questionnaire design is a primary contributor to nonsampling errors—specifically, response errors—the questionnaire should be well designed. The questions should minimize the possibility that respondents will give inaccurate answers. The questions asked are the basic essence of a research project. Inquiring by way of interrogation through specific questions forms the basic core of SURVEY RESEARCH. The reliability and validity of survey results are dependent on the way the specific questions are planned, constructed, and executed.

Constructing a questionnaire that generates accurate data which are relevant to solving the research problem is not a simple matter. A questionnaire can flow well from part to part, contain questions easily understood by respondents, address the issues identified in the study's research objectives, and lend itself to the appropriate analytical techniques, but may totally fail to present an accurate picture of reality conducive to making decisions that lead to a solution of the management problem. How is this possible? A questionnaire is more than just a series of well-worded questions. It is a totality, a system in which each part is vital to every other part of the whole instrument.

Goals of a Questionnaire

Researchers should take great care in designing this data-collection instrument. A good questionnaire should accomplish the following goals:

Contextualize the Information Collected

The researcher should include any questions that will aid in the interpretation of those questions that are directly related to the research objectives. In other words, include questions that can be used by the decision maker in the decision-making process, even if those additional questions are not directly related to the research objectives. A questionnaire is more than merely a conversion of research objectives into survey questions.

Express the Study Objectives in Question Form

The questionnaire must capture the essence of the study objectives and ask questions that will gather the data that will provide the information needed to answer the various research issues. Quite often, a set of study objectives is adapted to an existing questionnaire that has been effective in the past. Each project with its unique set of study objectives should have a custom-made questionnaire designed especially for that project. The design of the questionnaire is the wrong place to try to economize during the research process.

Measure the Attitude, Behavior, Intention, Attributes, or Other Characteristics of the Respondent

The questions must be specific and reported in a form that will allow for comparisons to be made and results to be analyzed. The responses to the questions must provide the information that is necessary to answer the research questions and in a format that can be subjected to the appropriate analytical technique.

Create Harmony and Rapport with the Respondent

A well-designed questionnaire targeted at the correct population sample should provide an enjoyable experience for the respondent. The frame of reference of the respondent must be considered in the design, wording, and sequencing of a questionnaire. Occupational jargon, cultural background, educational level, and regional differences can alter the effectiveness of a questionnaire if they are not taken into consideration. Not only should the questionnaire appeal to the respondent, it should be designed so the respondent can easily understand it, be able to answer it, and be willing to answer it.

Provide Just the Right Amount of Information: No More, No Less

This is a trite statement, but it has much truth to it. Opinions differ on just how much information is needed to answer a set of research questions. However, in designing a questionnaire the two basic mistakes are leaving an important question unasked, which makes the survey incomplete, and asking too many irrelevant questions, which makes the survey too long and unwieldy. A researcher must learn to economize in asking questions to avoid respondent burnout, which leads to early termination and incomplete and inaccurate information. However, care must be taken in the design process to be sure the quantity of information is gathered to accomplish the research objectives.

Designing a Questionnaire

Many methods are accepted for designing a questionnaire. Various research texts suggest procedures ranging from four to fourteen sequential steps. Questionnaire design, no matter how formalized, still requires a measure of science and a measure of art with a good dose of humility mixed in. In designing a questionnaire, presumption must be set aside. Although for simplicity of format, the sequence for developing a questionnaire is given on a step-by-step basis, rarely is a questionnaire constructed in such a routine way. Quite often it is necessary to skip from one step to another and to loop back through a previous series of steps.

The following steps represent a sequential procedure that needs to be considered for the development of an effective survey instrument.

> *Step 1:* Determine the specific information needed to achieve the research objectives.
> *Step 2:* Identify the sources of the required information.
> *Step 3:* Choose the method of administration that suits the information required and the sources of information.
> *Step 4:* Determine the types of questions to be used and form of response.
> *Step 5:* Develop the specific questions to be asked.
> *Step 6:* Determine the sequence of the questions and the length of the questionnaire.
> *Step 7:* Predetermine coding.
> *Step 8:* Pretest the questionnaire.
> *Step 9:* Review and revise the questionnaire

SUGGESTED READING

Stevens, Robert E., Bruce Wrenn, Morris E. Ruddick, and Philip K. Sherwood, *The Marketing Research Guide* (Binghamton, NY: The Haworth Press), 1997.

RESEARCH DESIGN

A research design is similar to a road map—you can see where you currently are, where you want to be at the completion of your journey, and can determine the best (most efficient and effective) route to take to get to your destination. We may have to take unforeseen detours along the way, but by keeping our ultimate objective constantly in mind and using our map we can arrive at our destination. Our research purpose and objectives suggest which route (design) might be best to get us where we want to go, but there is more than one way to "get there from here." Choice of research design is not like solving a problem in algebra where there is only one correct answer and an infinite number of wrong ones. Choice of research design is more like selecting a cheesecake recipe—some are better than others but there is no one that is universally accepted as "best." Successfully completing a research project consists of making those choices that will fulfill the research purpose and obtain answers to the research questions in an efficient and effective manner.

Choice of design type is not determined by the nature of the strategic decision faced by the administrator such that we would use research design A whenever we need to evaluate the extent of a new ministry opportunity, or design B when deciding on which of two advertising programs to run. Rather, choice of research design is influenced by a number of variables such as the decision maker's attitude toward risk, the types of decisions being faced, the size of the research budget, time frame, the nature of the research objectives, and other subtle and not-so-subtle factors. Much of the choice, however, will depend upon the fundamental objective implied by the research question.

- To conduct a general *exploration* of the issue, gain some broad insights into the phenomenon, and achieve a better "feel" for the subject under investigation.
- To *describe* a population, event, or phenomenon in a precise manner where we can attach numbers to represent the extent to which something occurs or determine the degree two or more variables covary.
- To attribute *cause* and effect relationships among two or more variables so that we can better understand and predict the outcome of one variable when varying another.

These three broadly different objectives give us the names of our three categories of research designs: exploratory, descriptive, and causal. EXPLORATORY RESEARCH is usually called for if the management problem is vague or can be only broadly defined. Research at this stage may involve a variety of techniques (literature review, focus groups, in-depth interviews, psychoanalytic studies, and case studies) and is characterized by the flexibility allowed to researchers in the exploration of relevant issues. DESCRIPTIVE RESEARCH is conducted when there is a need to measure the frequency with which a sampled population behaves, thinks, or is likely to act or to determine the extent to which two variables covary. Research must be highly structured in descriptive research so that any variation in the variables under investigation can be attributed to differences in the respondents rather than to variations in the questioning, which is acceptable in exploratory research. Causal research is also highly structured, and includes exercise of control over variables in order to test cause-and-effect relationships between variables. Exploratory research is used to generate hypotheses, and both descriptive and causal research are used to test hypotheses.

SUGGESTED READING

Wrenn, Bruce, Robert Stevens, David Loudon, *Marketing Research* (Binghamton, NY: The Haworth Press), 2002.

RESEARCH METHODOLOGY

Research methodology refers to the steps or sequence of events needed to plan what marketing data are to be collected, from whom, and how they are to be analyzed. Research methodology is part of the overall marketing research process shown in the following outline:

1. Define the management problem
2. State research objectives
3. Develop research methodology
   a. Define specific information needs
   b. Define population to be studied
   c. Develop sampling technique and determine sample size
   d. Determine how to measure variables or attributes to be studied
   e. Determine how to collect data
   f. Determine how to analyze data

4. Collect data
5. Analyze and interpret data
6. Present findings

The first step in developing the research methodology is to identify the specific types of information needed to accomplish the research objectives. Although this might appear to be an inherent part of the process of developing the objectives, it is usually wise to approach this in a more formal way by identifying specific information types. For example, let's say a research objective was stated as follows: Identify the characteristics of heavy donors, light donors, and non-donors to a ministry organization. The word "characteristic" can take on a wide variety of definitions—socioeconomic, psychological, behavioral, and physical. What specific types of information are needed in this particular research project? Answering this question forces the researcher to evaluate information sought with objectives and the management problem in mind. This step could be completed under the measurement area—deciding what is to be measured—and this is acceptable. However, since every aspect of research methodology is directly influenced by the type of information to be collected and analyzed, there are advantages to using this as the initial step in methodology.

The other steps in developing the research methodology follow the definition of information needs. The research population, sampling methods and size, measurement, data collection, and analysis are all based on the types of information to be collected.

SAMPLING

Sampling refers to the process of selecting individuals or organizations from which to collect data. Two separate decisions are called for in this step. The first is to determine how specific sample elements will be drawn from the population. The approach selected depends on the nature of the problem and the nature of the population under study. For probability sample designs, the objective is to draw a sample that is both representative and useful. For nonprobability designs, the objective is to select a useful sample even though it may not be representative of the population. The sample design influences the applicability of various types of analysis; some types of analysis are directly dependent upon how sample elements are drawn.

Sample elements must be drawn from a sampling frame (i.e., a list of all the elements in the population). Building such a list is a basic need for most organizations. Many churches have no formal technique to list even their own members much less other constituent groups.

The sampling frame should include all members of the population. Failure to meet this requirement can result in bias. If, for example, you were trying to determine the number of families of a town who were unchurched and were going to use the telephone book as your list of families to call, three problems would be encountered. First, not everyone has a land-line telephone; and, some of those who do not tend to be in a low-income bracket. Second, 15 to 20 percent of phone owners have unlisted numbers. Third, new residents would not be listed. The difference between your list (telephone book) and area residents could be substantial and could bias the results.

Sample size represents the other side of the decision. Determining how many sample elements are needed to accomplish the research objectives requires both analysis and judgment. Such things as costs, response rate, and homogeneity of sample elements must be considered when deciding on sample size. In some studies, the cost may dictate the sample size.

SCALES

The term "scale" can refer to the method of expressing the value or magnitude by numbers (i.e., a nominal, ordinal, interval, or ratio scale), or the measuring device itself (e.g., a Likert, semantic differential, Thurstone, or rank-order scale). We will refer to it in the latter sense here.

No one scaling device is considered best under all measurement circumstances. We will discuss the most commonly used scales along with some guidelines for their use. The following are some commonly used scales to measure variables of interest for religious marketers.

ATTITUDES

Strongly Agree	Agree	Neither Agree nor Disagree	Disagree	Strongly Disagree
5	4	3	2	1

PERFORMANCE OR QUALITY

Excellent	Very Good	Good	Fair	Poor
5	4	3	2	1

SATISFACTION

Completely Satisfied		Very Satisfied		Fairly Well Satisfied		Somewhat Dissatisfied	Dissatis-fied	Very Dissastisfied	Unsatis-fied
10	9	8	7	6	5	4	3	2	1

IMPORTANCE

Of Critical Importance	Very Important	Somewhat Important	Of Little Importance	Not at All Important
5	4	3	2	1

EXPERIENCE

Far Exceeded My Expectations	Exceeded My Expectations	Met My Expectations	Did Not Meet My Expectations	Far Below My Expectations
5	4	3	2	1

INTENTION

Extremely Likely	Very Likely	Somewhat Likely	About 50-50 Chance	Somewhat Unlikely	Very Unlikely	Extremely Unlikely
7	6	5	4	3	2	1

BEHAVIOR

Always	Frequently	Occasionally	Infrequently	Not At All
5	4	3	2	1

FREQUENCY

More Than Once a Week	About Once a Week	Two or Three Times a Month	About Once a Month	Less Than Once a Month	Almost Never	Never
7	6	5	4	3	2	1

Several choices confront the researcher using one of these scales.

1. *The number of item statements and scale points.* Research indicates that scale reliability improves, up to a point, with increases in the number of item statements and scale points. So, for example, a questionnaire that uses twelve attitude item statements is more reliable than one that uses only three item statements, but thirty item statements is probably less reliable than twelve. Why? Because of the fatigue factor—respondents get fatigued in answering too many questions and their responses are made more to "get it over with" rather than as a true representation of their state of mind. The same is true for response points on the scale—five is better than three, but more than ten points does not improve reliability. Typically, the number of scale points varies between five to seven.

2. *Odd or even number of points.* Is a scale with an even number of points preferable to an odd number, or is the odd number preferable? No hard evidence supports either choice. The odd number provides a midpoint on the scale, while the even number forces respondents to "choose sides" (lean toward one end of the scale or the other). This remains a matter of research preference.

3. *Use of "don't know" and "no opinion."* The general tendency for interviewers is to discourage respondents from choosing a "don't know" or "no opinion" option when responding to a scaled item statement. Many respondents then select the midpoint of an odd-number scale as the default option. Obviously, researchers analyzing the data are then unable to determine how many people marked "3" on the five-point scale because that expressed the intensity with which they held an attitude, and how many marked "3" because they did not know how they felt, and chose the midpoint because it was the safest option available. These kinds of compromises to the validity of the instrument argue persuasively for a scale that provides for both a "don't know" and a "no opinion" option for respondents, and for instructions to interviewers to accept these responses from respondents.

Researchers who plan to use specific analytical techniques to test hypotheses or determine the relationship between variables of interest (e.g., what best explains level of satisfaction with a particular ministry among members of a target audience) must have collected data using the appropriate scale for that technique. In other words, the scale used must generate the data in the form required by the statistical process being used to analyze the results—not all scales will generate data in the proper form. Consequently, the wise researcher will anticipate how the data need to be analyzed when designing the data-collection instrument, not after the data have been collected.

SECONDARY DATA

RESEARCH DESIGN is the "road map" for the researcher, indicating the route he or she will take in collecting the information to ultimately solve the problem or evaluate the opportunity in question. The types of data collected in executing this research design will be either primary data or secondary data. PRIMARY DATA are those that are collected for the first time by the researcher for the specific research project at hand. Secondary data are data previously gathered for some other purpose.

Secondary data can be used in several ways, even though the research design might require the use of primary data. The most common uses are:

1. In some cases the information and insights gained from secondary data are sufficient to answer the research questions.
2. Secondary data can provide the background necessary to understand the problem situation and provide an overview of the market dynamics.
3. Secondary data often can provide exploratory information that can aid in the planning and design of the instruments used to gather primary data.
4. Secondary data can serve as a check and standard for evaluating primary data.
5. Secondary data can give insight into sample selection.
6. Secondary data can suggest research hypotheses or ideas that can be studied in the primary data phase of the research process.

The extensive use of secondary data reduces the possibility of "reinventing the wheel" by gathering primary data that someone else has already collected.

Disadvantages of Secondary Data

Since secondary data, both internal and external, were generated for some purpose other than to answer the research question at hand, care must be taken in their application. The limitations of secondary data must be considered. Secondary data have the following potential limitations or disadvantages:

1. *A poor "fit."* The secondary data collected for some other research objective or purpose may not be relevant to the research question at hand. In most cases, the secondary data will not adequately fit the problem. In other cases, secondary data collected from various sources will not be in the right intervals, unit of measurement or categories for proper cross-comparison. The secondary data may not be collected from the correct or most representative sample frame.

2. *Accuracy.* The question of accuracy takes several things into consideration. First of all, there is the question of whether the secondary data came from a primary or secondary source. Secondary sources of secondary data should be avoided. The next consideration is the organization or agency that originally collected the data. What is the quality of the organization's methodology and data-gathering design? What is its reputation for credibility?

3. *Age.* A major problem with published and secondary data is the timeliness of the information. Old information is not necessarily bad information; however, in many dynamic markets, up-to-date information is an absolute necessity.

4. *Quality.* Information quality is sometimes unknown. The reputation and capability of the collecting agency is important to assessing the quality of the information provided. To verify the overall quality of secondary information, it may be necessary to know how the data were collected, what the sampling plan was, what data-collection method was used, what field procedures were utilized, what training was provided, what degree of non-response was experienced, and what other sources of error are possible.

Secondary Data Sources

The first problem that confronts a researcher in initiating a secondary data search is the massive amount, wide variety, and many locations of secondary data. Some method of logically summarizing the sources of secondary data is helpful. Most textbooks on the subject divide secondary data sources into two groups: (1) internal data sources, and (2) external data sources.

Internal secondary data sources are closest at hand since they are found within the organization initiating the research process. These internal data have been collected for other purposes but are available to be consolidated, compared, and analyzed to answer the new research question being posed. This is particularly true of organizations that have sophisticated management information systems that routinely gather and consolidate useful marketing, accounting, and membership information.

Even though most research projects require more than just internal data, this is a very cost-efficient place to begin the data search. Quite often a review of all internal secondary data sources will inexpensively give direction for the next phase of data collection. The internal search will give clues to what external data sources are required to gather the information needed to answer the research question.

External secondary data originate outside the confines of the organization. An overwhelming number of external sources of data are available to the researcher. Good external secondary data may be found through libraries, Internet searches, associations, and general guides to secondary data. The *Directory of Directories* and the *Encyclopedia of Associations* are excellent sources for finding associations and organizations that may provide secondary information for a particular industry.

The Web has become the first, and too often the only, source to be used by the marketing researcher in search of pertinent secondary data. It is reasonable to assume that the reader of this book has had experience "surfing the Web," and therefore is familiar with Web browsers (e.g., Netscape or Microsoft Internet Explorer); search engines or portals (e.g., AltaVista, Infoseek, HotBot, Google, Excite, Yahoo!, etc.); indexes of periodical literature (e.g., EBSCOhost and ATLA Religion Database); Web search strategies (e.g., use of parentheses, and/or, +, −, quotation marks, asterisk, etc.); and use of newsgroups (i.e., Internet sites where people can post queries or respond to other people's queries or post comments. Over 250,000 newsgroups exist, each devoted to a specific topic). The savvy researcher can harness these and other resources and methods of using the Internet to discover relevant secondary data available over the Internet. The following are some useful Web sites for religious organizations:

www.mra-net.org

The Marketing Research Association's site includes the latest edition of their Blue Book and a listing of research firms in the United States. Also, they have links to other marketing research sites, a newsgroup where researchers can post items of interest to other researchers, and an events calendar.

www.marketingpower.com

The American Marketing Association includes a variety of resources for marketers and marketing researches with links to other marketing related sites.

www.church-marketing.com

Church Marketing Solutions was established to educate churches on the basic process of marketing as well as provide church marketing resources.

SURVEY RESEARCH

Surveys are frequently used to collect all the types of PRIMARY DATA. Surveys generate data that make it possible to test various types of hypotheses that suggest relationships between those variables and between respondent groups. For example, we might use a survey to segment a target audience and then test hypotheses that some segments are more conservative than other segments, or that some segments acquire more information by using the Internet than other segments. A test of a hypothetical relationship between variables might involve determining the degree of influence a set of demographic, attitudinal, or behavioral variables had in explaining a target audience decision (e.g., membership in small groups in a church). Statistical analytical techniques to test such hypotheses require that the data being analyzed be collected through descriptive or causal data-collection methods, and most frequently the method for descriptive research is a survey.

Survey Methods

Descriptive research surveys can be conducted in a variety of ways using many combinations of people and electronics and conducted in a variety of locations. Table 6 displays a few of the types of survey delivery methods possible from such combinations.

Telephone Interviewing

Telephone interviewing is usually employed when the study design requires speedy collection of information from a large, geographically dispersed population that would be too costly to do in person; when eligibility is difficult (necessitating many contacts for a completed interview); when the questionnaire is relatively short; or when face-to-face contact is not necessary.

TABLE 6. Survey Delivery Method

Location of Interaction	Telephone	Mail	Personal	Computer or Fax
Home	WATS or IVR	Self-administered or panels	Door-to-door	Internet or disk by mail
Work	WATS or IVR	Self-administered or lock box	Executive interview	Internet or fax
Malls	—	—	Mall intercept	Computer-assisted
Central location research facility	—	—	On-site	Computer-assisted

Note: IVR = Interactive Voice Response; WATS = Wide-Area Telephone Service.

Mail Surveys

Mail surveys are commonly used in either ad hoc (one time) or mail panel research. In ad hoc research projects a sample of respondents is chosen to be representative of the population of interest and a questionnaire is sent by mail. The mail questionnaire may be preceded by and/or followed by a telephone call intended to encourage participation. The combination of telephone and mail is an attempt to reduce the high rate of nonresponse that plagues ad hoc, and to a lesser degree, mail panel surveys.

Personal Interviewing

This face-to-face method is employed when the survey may be too long to conduct over the telephone or there might be material to show the respondent. Personal interviews are effective when the sample necessitates contacting homes in a specific manner, such as every fourth home or going to every home until an interview is conducted, then skipping a specified number of homes before attempting the next contact as well as other applications.

Personal interviews allow for more in-depth probing on various issues and are the most productive, accurate, comprehensive, controlled, and versatile types of communication. The well-trained interviewer has ample opportunity to probe and interpret body language, facial expression, and other nuances during the interaction. Rapport can be developed that would put the interviewee at ease and gain his or her cooperation. The interviewer can explain any misunderstanding the respondent might have and keep the respondent on track and in sequence in responding to the questionnaire. In spite of the advantages of greater depth and productivity, the personal interview does take more time and money to administer.

Internet Research

Internet surveys can either be e-mail or Web-based approaches. E-mail surveys are simple to compose and send, but are limited to simple text (i.e., flat text format); allow for limited visual presentations (e.g., no photo or video-based stimuli) and interactive capabilities; and cannot permit complex skip patterns.

Web surveys, in comparison, are in HTML format and offer much more flexibility to the researcher, providing opportunity for presentation of complex audio and visual stimuli such as animation, photos, and video clips; interaction with respondent; skip patterns; use of color; pop-up instructions to provide help with questions; and drop-down boxes to allow respondents to choose from long lists of possible answers (e.g., "In which state do you currently reside?"). Based on answers to a set of screening questions, Web-based Internet surveys can direct respondents to customized survey questions specifically designed with those respondents' characteristics in mind. These types of HTML format surveys can also be downloaded to the respondent's computer for completion and then either mailed or electronically sent to another researcher. Of course differences in monitor screen size, computer clock speed, use of full or partial screen for viewing questionnaire, use of broadband versus telephone transmission lines, etc., may result in different presentations of the questionnaire for different viewers. Also, computer navigation skills still vary widely across the population and must be taken into account when designing a Web-based survey.

SUGGESTED READING

Alreck, Pamela L. and Robert T. Settle, *The Survey Research Handbook* (Chicago: Irwin), 1995.
Dillman, Don, *Mail and Internet Surveys* (New York: John Wiley and Sons), 2000.

SWOT ANALYSIS

A SWOT analysis is an acronym for an evaluation of **s**trengths, **w**eaknesses, **o**pportunities, and **t**hreats of an organization. The strengths and weaknesses are internal to the organization, and the opportunities and threats deal with the external environment over which the organization has no control. A SWOT analysis helps an organization develop strategies to achieve its goals.

Strengths can be thought of as positive traits or competitive advantages. New, well-designed, and attractive physical facilities may be a strength. A weakness is a competitive disadvantage. For example, a small church may not be well known in its area; very little public awareness could be considered a weakness.

An opportunity is a situation outside of the organization that may positively affect the organization, and a threat is a situation outside of the organization that may negatively affect the organization. These situations include cultural trends, competitive activities, and economic and social conditions. The following is an example of a SWOT analysis.

Strengths	Extremely committed and active membership
	An outstanding pastor
	A strong financial condition with no debt
Weaknesses	A poor location
	Dilapidated physical facilities
	Public awareness
Opportunities	Strong economy
	Large, growing population in the area
	Closure of three other area churches
Threats	Opening of new church across the street
	Unpopular decisions by denomination's national headquarters
	New requirements of local government building codes

Since the SWOT analysis is used to help develop strategy, a church should make an effort to ensure that the SWOT is accurate. Based on the SWOT example previously listed, this church may make a strategic decision to change locations. However, if the SWOT is not accurate, poor strategy obviously could be developed. Leaders will often have different perceptions of the SWOT. When these differences exist, member surveys and market research should be conducted in an effort to gather valid and reliable information.

TARGET AUDIENCE

Target audience refers to the specific group of constituents toward which marketing communications are directed. Communication can be targeted toward many potential audiences. When the communication is directed toward members, it is referred to as internal communications. External communications are used when the effort is directed toward potential members, the public at large, or supporters who are not members. Normally, organizations promote to both groups so it is not an either/or decision, but one of relative emphasis.

Different audiences are going to be interested in different information, so great care must be exercised in providing the right information to the right group. If a religious organization is undertaking a new mission project, for example, past supporters do not need the same type of information that new potential supporters do. The information already held by past supporters is different from that of potential supporters. The frames of reference for the two groups are different. Church members may know what the annual church picnic involves, but visitors do not. Information sent to the two groups should reflect this.

One basic approach to recognizing the differences in target audiences is to develop a profile of each potential audience. This means listing characteristics such as age, sex, religious affiliation, stage in the family life cycle, etc. The resulting profile is then used to determine what messages to send to each group but also the best media to use to reach the target audience.

Appendix A

Marketing and Religion: A Review of the Two Literatures

Bruce Wrenn
Phylis Mansfield

INTRODUCTION

Marketing's "identity crisis" was relatively short-lived in the late 1960s and 1970s as marketing theorists debated first, how far the application of marketing should extend (Kotler and Levy, 1969; Luck, 1969; Nickels, 1974; Arndt, 1978), and second, what exactly distinguishes marketing from all the other disciplines from which it borrows (e.g., economics, psychology, sociology, anthropology, etc.) (cf. Hunt, 1983). Exchange in all its forms became the central organizing theory that defined marketing as a discipline, leading to acceptance of the broadened application of marketing to not-for-profit fields such as education, the arts, health care, social causes, and politics, as well as to professional services within the commercial arena.

The initial challenge to the application of marketing to these areas primarily centered around whether marketing really "worked" in such nontraditional fields, and the degree to which marketing practice must be modified to be useful in these applications. Articles such as Berry's (1980) "Services Marketing Is Different," attempted to demonstrate that marketing could indeed be of value in a broadened application, but required modification to make its optimal contribution. Practitioners in these areas may have been initially skeptical about how useful marketing would prove to be, but were open to persuasion if it could be demonstrated that marketing could help them achieve their objectives. Any serious philosophical musings on the extension of marketing theory was confirmed to marketing theorists, and was relatively quickly dispatched. The latest (last?) arena for the exten-

Reprinted from *The Journal of Ministry Marketing & Management*, The Haworth Press, Inc., 2002, 7(1), 61-80.

sion of marketing—religious organizations—promises to be different from other not-for-profit applications.

The application of marketing theory and practice to religious organizations has not been without controversy. The presence of a journal *(Journal of Ministry Marketing & Management)* devoted to scholarship on the topic, and the publication of numerous books and articles providing extensive "how-to" advice on the application of marketing to churches and other religious institutions would imply that the acceptance of the idea of marketing's use by such organizations is widespread, if not universal. However, other evidence argues differently. The backlash against marketing by some theologians and other critics has, in fact, differed by degree and nature from that which accompanied the proposed use of marketing by not-for-profit organizations in the late 1960s. The time appears ripe for a review of the literature, both pro and con, to determine how thought has evolved on the topic from its origins to the beginning of a new century.

ORIGINS OF RELIGIOUS ORGANIZATIONAL MARKETING

Any attempt to conduct an etymological study of "religious marketing" will encounter a dilemma similar to that identified by Bartels (1976) in his *The History of Marketing Thought*—is it religious marketing *thought* or religious marketing *practice* that is being chronicled? Bartels points out that the term "marketing" was first used as a noun, in contrast to its earlier use as a verb, sometime between 1906 and 1911. There can be no doubt, however, that the practice of what we now refer to as marketing began long before the twentieth century. (Bartels maintains marketing in this sense has *always* existed, p. 3.)

The same difficulty occurs when one attempts to identify the provenance of religious marketing, since some have claimed that marketing practices have always accompanied the spread of religion. Witness what one proponent of the application of marketing to churches has declared: "The Bible is one of the world's great marketing texts" (Barna 1988, p. 29).

In America, historians have maintained that "marketing" practices were used by preachers at least as far back as colonial times. Stout (1991) described George Whitefield, a famous evangelist during the Great Awakening of the 1730s-1740s, as presenting religion as "a product that could be marketed" (p. 35). Like Bartels, however, we must distinguish between the practice and the conception of marketing (Bartels refers to the need to focus on the "concept of a practice"). That is, at what point did the practice become identified as "marketing" in the literature?

Early Literature

The earliest example of "marketing-like" thought applied to religion in the literature might be Jay Benson Hamilton's book, *Empty Churches and How to Fill Them,* published in 1879. Beginning in the early part of the twentieth century, books began to appear that described how to promote the church, such as:

Principles of Successful [sic] Advertising (Stelzle, 1908)
Advertising the Church (Ellis, 1913)
Church Publicity: The Modern Way to Compel Them to Come In (Reisner, 1913)
How to Fill the Pews (Elliot, 1917)
Church Advertising: Its Why and How (Ashley, 1917)
How to Advertise a Church (Elliot, 1920)
Handbook of Church Advertising (Case, 1921)
Church and Sunday School Publicity (Smith, 1922)

This interest in the use of advertising for religious organizations coincided with the formative period for advertising thought in general in the United States (Bartels, 1976). This coincidence of formative marketing thought and its immediate application to religious organizations is emblematic of the fervor with which some religious leaders adopt any techniques capable of increasing the effectiveness of spreading religious beliefs throughout the population. John Wesley's declaration that "I would observe every punctilio or order, except when the salvation of souls is at stake. Then I prefer the end to the means" (quoted in Ensley, 1958, p. 38) embodies this philosophy of adopting "whatever works" with little concern for the theoretical or theological issues of *appropriateness*. As we will see, the sharp division of opinion between those who so value the ends that they are less concerned with debating the particulars of the means, from those who believe that such uncritical acceptance of modernity runs counter to religious tradition and propriety is a common theme in the current religious marketing literature. Early application of marketing tools to religious organizations however, leaned more toward adoption of the "whatever works" school of thought.

Contemporary Literature

The early literature, as previously discussed, concentrated on the use of marketing tools, primarily promotion, for religious organizations. In the later half of the twentieth century we see the term "marketing," rather than promotion or publicity, gain currency in its application to religion. This change in terminology reflects the ascendancy of the marketing concept as a core construct for marketing theory (cf. Wrenn, 1997, for a chronology of the marketing concept in marketing literature). The marketing concept's focus on customer needs and consumer sovereignty will become a major focal point of the opponents of marketing in religious circles. This clash of philosophies (the marketing concept is often referred to as a philosophy—see Houston 1986) between marketers and theologians necessitates separating the marketing and religious literature devoted to the subject.

Marketing Literature

The first article written in support of the use of marketing by religious organizations was entitled "A Marketing Analysis of Religion," written by James Culliton (1959), Dean of the College of Commerce at the University of Notre Dame. A review of the marketing literature by Cutler (1991) revealed that in the next thirty years only thirty-five articles were written on the application of marketing for religious institutions. Most of these articles appeared in conference proceedings, case books, or *Marketing News.* Nearly 80 percent of the articles were published in the 1980s. The 1990s have seen increased interest in the topic by marketing scholars, and the birth of a journal, the *Journal of Ministry Marketing and Management,* provided increased coverage of religious marketing scholarship. (See Table 7 for a listing of the conceptual marketing literature and Table 8 for the empirical marketing literature on the topic.)

The stance taken by these marketing writers has been, as might be expected, almost entirely supportive of the use of marketing by religious organizations, with the only cautionary note voiced by Wrenn and Saliba (1993, 1995). Hirschman (1983) in her article "Aesthetics, Ideologies and the Limits of the Marketing Concept," classified religious groups as ideologies and discussed why the marketing concept does not apply to such entities. However, the scope of her thesis was much broader than just religious groups, and is therefore not included in Table 7.

Attention has been given to development of an economic theory of religion (Hull and Bold, 1989; Iannaccone, 1992) and to a rational choice theory of religious (Stark and Bainbridge, 1987) or religious practice as social exchange (cf. Lee, 1992, for a review of this literature). Although marketing theorists have also applied these theoretical models to the study of marketing, there is no overlap of marketing, religion, and these theoretical models therefore this literature is not included in Table 7. Neither will we include the literature on religious conversion models (cf. Kilbourne and Richardson, 1988), which parallels marketing consumer behavior theory, but which has not been the subject of marketing inquiry per se.

TABLE 7. Conceptual Articles in the Marketing Literature

Author/Date	Purpose	Key Words	Stance	Use/Source	Comments
Dunlap and Rountree, 1982	Describe how marketing concepts can be applied to churches	Marketing concept, Church	Promarketing	Application; Case study	Discusses why marketing is needed by religious organizations; several case studies of how churches use marketing
LeMasters, 1988	Examine differences in religious organizations and other nonprofits in use of marketing	Nonprofit, Church marketing	Promarketing	Application	Describes reasons for suspicion of marketing by religious organization leaders
Wrenn and Saliba, 1988	Describe how one denomination has used geodemography	Geodemography, Segmentation, Target marketing	Promarketing	Application; Case study	Describes how the Seventh Day Adventist Church has used geodemographic data to segment and target ministries
Cutler, 1991	Literature review	Literature review	Neutral	NA	Review of literature on marketing of religion; primarily from proceedings and other marketing literature
Wrenn, 1992	Describe church services within a product mix portfolio format	Product portfolio, Product mix, Mission	Promarketing	Application	Identifies the dimensions useful for organizing a portfolio of church services; demonstrates how churches can target different services to individuals
Wrenn, 1993a	Describe role marketing can play for religious organizations	Marketing, Religious organizations	Promarketing	Theoretical	Suggests appropriate role of marketing for religious organizations; List of distinctive characteristics of religious organizational marketing
Wrenn, 1993b	Describe application of "customer service" to religious organizations	Customer Service, Churches, Moments of truth	Promarketing	Application	Depth application of business principles to generate congregation satisfaction. Describes Jan Carlson's "moments of truth"
Wrenn and Saliba, 1993	Addresses objections of religious leaders to use of marketing	Nature of religion, Marketing	Promarketing	Theoretical	Not everything religious organizations do is marketable, but some things are

TABLE 7 (continued)

Author/Date	Purpose	Key Words	Stance	Use/Source	Comments
Considine, 1995a	Applies marketing concept to churches	Marketing concept, Customer orientation	Promarketing	Application	Reviews special challenges to churches; Why people do not attend; Uses marketing concept
Considine, 1995b	Examine the state of marketing research use in churches	Marketing research, Ministry research, Exploratory research, Data analysis	Promarketing	Application, Case Studies	Uses case studies to describe how churches can use marketing research techniques
Wrenn, 1995	Apply internal marketing concept to church membership	Internal marketing, Market orientation, Church membership	Promarketing	Application	Suggestions for how a church can implement a member service program
Wrenn and Saliba, 1995	Defines areas where religious marketing is different from other not-for-profit marketing	Religious marketing, Not-for-profit	Promarketing	Theoretical	Identifies role of marketing for religious organizations and how it is substantially different from other not-for-profits and for-profit firms
Wrenn et al., 1995	Apply marketing philosophy and marketing orientation to ministry	Marketing concept, Customer orientation, Marketing philosophy, Ministry marketing	Promarketing	Application, Case Studies	Discusses four main approaches to ministry in the U.S., production, sales, market, and societal market
Clinton et al., 1996	Explore uses of marketing research in churches	Attitude surveys, Statistical analysis, Constituent research	Promarketing	Application	How-to on doing research in church constituencies, including sampling; Brief description of data analysis techniques
Considine, 1996a	Examine characteristics of "baby boomers" as related to church needs	Baby boomers, Church marketing, Target marketing, Strategic marketing	Promarketing	Application	Lists ten traits common to churches who are reaching baby boomer population

Citation	Purpose	Topics	Stance	Type	Description
Considine, 1996b	Explore use of market segmentation in churches	Market segmentation, Niche marketing, Church marketing, Church growth	Promarketing	Application	Encourages churches to utilize concepts of segmentation; Discusses strategies used by growing churches
Hines, 1996b	Examine uses for publicity in churches	News releases, Church publicity, Promotion, Communication	Promarketing	Application	How-to on using publicity in church environment; Getting articles published
Muncy, 1996	Examine use of target segmentation in churches	Church growth, Market differentiation, Target marketing	Promarketing	Application	Discusses different methods of target segmentation; Family life cycle as one method
Wymer, 1997	Discuss recruitment and retention of volunteers	Church volunteers, Administration, Segmentation, Recruiting, Retention	Promarketing	Application	Discusses recruitment and retention of church volunteers from a marketing management perspective; Segmentation into types of volunteers
Murray, 1997	Investigates donor appeal sensitivity	Content Analysis, Trends Analysis, Donor information, Ministry marketing	Promarketing	Application, Case studies	Applies demographics to donor appeal preferences; Content analysis of donor appeal types
Primeaux et al., 1997	Develop a survey to measure parishioner satisfaction	Community, Likert, Participation organization, Survey	Promarketing	Application	Scale development for "Parishioner satisfaction"; twenty-eight items; four factors crucial to satisfaction—community, communication, contribution, and communion
Wymer, 1998	Develop strategies for recruitment and retention of church volunteers	Church volunteers, Recruitment, Retention, Church marketing	Promarketing	Application	Examines 4 Ps of marketing as applied to church volunteers
Considine, 1999	Examine appropriateness of promotion styles for churches	Church marketing, Promotion, Direct mail, Publicity	Promarketing	Application	Considers newspaper, TV in certain cases inappropriate; Church can use any promotion strategy but must match goal to strategy's outcome

TABLE 7 (continued)

Author/Date	Purpose	Key Words	Stance	Use/Source	Comments
Cutler and Winans, 1999	Document the attitude of religion scholars toward marketing	Church marketing, Religion, Nonprofit marketing, Religious organizations	Neutral	NA	Review of religion literature; Reasons for religious institutions' resistance to marketing as well as gradual acceptance are discussed
Horne and McAuley, 1999	Explore application of marketing to church services	Marketing, Nonprofit, Customer values, Customer exchanges	Promarketing	Application	Applies customer exchange process to churches; Church marketing is complicated in terms of brand identity, product offerings, and target audience
Wymer, 1999a	Examine segmentation for church groups	Small group ministries, leadership, teaching styles	Promarketing	Application	Segments potential congregation/participants and their needs into small groups through market segmentation and market orientation
Joseph and Webb, 2000	Discuss advertising and promotional strategies for churches	Marketing church, Promotion, Church advertising, Member retention	Promarketing	Application	Model of church's publics and markets; For recruiting members using personal contact or referrals; limit mass media; For retention using personal referrals and print media; Mass media not useful for retention
Wymer, 2000	Review social psychology theory applied to churches	Youth ministry, Teaching, Persuasion, Inoculation theory	Promarketing	Application	Youth should be equipped to maintain Christian beliefs when faced with opposing message from popular culture; Program content more important than structure or format of program in retaining youth

TABLE 8. Empirical Articles in the Marketing Literature

Author/Date	Purpose	Key Words	Sample	Findings
Ginter and Talarzyk, 1978	Apply marketing concept to religious instruction	New product, Marketing concept	464 pastors; 697 lay members of Methodist Church in Ohio	Applied research; indicated which instructional packages should be developed
Dunlap et al., 1983	Assess attitudes of clergy toward marketing	Clergy, Marketing	144 clergy	Majority of clergy are positively inclined toward using marketing, although not familiar with concepts
Gazda et al., 1984	Assess the attitudes of clergy toward use of marketing by churches	Clergy, Marketing, Attitudes	144 clergy in California	65 percent of respondents felt the marketing of religion was necessary
McDaniel, 1986	Determine attitudes of clergy and public toward church advertising	Advertising, Church, Clergy	290 clergy; 261 public	Clergy have more favorable view of church advertising than does public
Moncrief et al., 1986	Survey clergy to determine knowledge and use of marketing	Clergy, Marketing practices	161 clergy	Clergy interested in applying business knowledge to church; 55 percent engage in marketing; 45 percent defined marketing as "meeting needs of customers"
Carman, 1987	Tests model for determining optimal promotion expenditures by churches	Advertising, Promotion, Decision models	2,064 Catholic adults in U.S.	Marketing analysis for not-for-profit organizations is very similar to that for for-profit organizations
Busenitz et al., 1990	Investigates use of general versus niche marketing strategies for churches	Strategies, Niche, Mass Marketing, Mission churches	226 Southern Baptist pastors	New churches achieving numerical growth in more highly saturated markets tend to use a more general approach to service offering
Mehta and Mehta, 1995	Identify factors that determine worshippers' satisfaction with church	Religious organization, Attitudes, Satisfaction	319 church or synagogue members	Satisfaction differed with denomination type; More satisfied were females, older members; frequent attendees; satisfaction correlated with higher donations

TABLE 8 (continued)

Author/Date	Purpose	Key Words	Sample	Findings
Stevens et al., 1995	Examine clergy views of marketing; five-year study	Marketing tools, Ministry Marketing, Clergy	102 clergy	Current study reveals more conservative (negative) attitudes toward marketing than five years previous
Zaleski and Zech, 1995	Analyze methods of solicitation and attitudes toward them	Fund-raising, Direct mail, Stewardship, Religious giving	523 Presbyterian households	Direct mail most successful with large groups; Professional fund-raiser effective with medium groups; Denominational material effective with small groups
Attaway et al., 1996	Identify consumers' importance ratings of fifteen church attributes	Market segmentation, Church marketing	424 individuals both churched and unchurched; 50 percent were students	Attribute importance differed by age group, gender, and stage in family life cycle
Hines, 1996a	Assess perceived effectiveness of advertising by churches	Church advertising, promotion, advertising effectiveness	Staff members of sixty-eight Southern Baptist churches	Ranked ten forms of advertising as to perceived effectiveness; Most effective were direct mail, TV, billboards; Least effective were yellow pages, newspaper church page, transit
Stevens et al., 1996	Study of factors that contribute to church commitment	Member commitment, Church commitment	166 members of two large Protestant denomination churches	Contributors to commitment included gender (female), age, length of membership, marital status (single), interdependence with others
Considine and Lepak, 1998	Investigate use of conjoint analysis to obtain church attribute preferences	Conjoint analysis, Church marketing, Preferences	Eighty-six MBA students; average age thirty years	This age group has strong preferences for messages in church that relate to life; additional programs
Sherman and Devlin, 1998	Examine clergy attitudes toward marketing activities	Marketing, Clergy, Ministry marketing	108 British clergy	Qualitative comments; Overall reluctance to accept use of marketing

Author/Date	Purpose	Key Concepts	Sample	Findings
Webb et al., 1998	Determine effectiveness of marketing communication efforts of pastors	Advertising, Promotion, Effectiveness, Membership	Sixty-four pastors of three mainline denominations	Marketing promotional tools vary in effectiveness for attracting new members versus retaining members; Personal contact is most effective for both attracting and retaining
White, 1998	Investigate application of two forms of advertising methods; mood manipulation and argument; Experiment	Church volunteers, Ministry marketing, Advertisement method	285 students from major Southeastern university	Both mood and ad argument play a major role in influencing individuals to donate time
Jones, 1999	Examine impact of pastor's leadership style on church growth	Shared vision, Innovation, Charisma	313 church board members from fifteen districts of Protestant churches	Most important factor in influencing church growth was pastor's shared vision with the congregation
Parker and Kent, 1999	Collect research data for church to use in planning	Church strategy, Church marketing, Research	464 members from one church congregation	Satisfaction with Sunday school and other areas of church differs by age group
Wymer, 1999b	Qualitative study of motives for volunteering in churches	Church volunteers, Motivation, Recruitment, Retention	1,013 Volunteers from forty churches in Midwest	Volunteers motivated by sense of duty; Retention best when volunteers are assimilated into volunteer community, receive feedback, and sense of accomplishment
Horne and Logie, 2000	Determine students' attitudes toward religious and moral education (RME)	Marketing, RME, Pupils	450 Scottish secondary-school children	RME has helped students to form their own view of the world and to learn skills of discussion and evaluation
Montgomery et al., 2000	Investigates attitudes of Generation X toward religion and spirituality	Religion, Marketing, Generation X	731 Generation Xers from four Metropolitan Statistical Areas (MSAs) in Southeastern U.S.	Significant differences of attitudes by gender and race or ethnicity; No difference based on parental status or education level
Saunders, 2000	Determine factors contributing to church member satisfaction	Retention, Satisfaction, Marketing	175 members of mainstream church in Midwest	Ten underlying dimensions of church member satisfaction; thirty-seven items total

Marketers have also written books on religious marketing that could be described largely as "how to" manuals on the subject (see Table 9). Writers of these promarketing articles and books usually took pains to make the point that they were not suggesting that religious institutions alter their core "product" (i.e., religious doctrine) to fit the needs of the marketplace. Rather, they indicated that marketing thought should, where appropriate, influence the ways the institutions structured their exchanges with "consumers." Empirical studies by marketers have indicated that as so described, marketing is seen positively by the clergy, who also indicate they make use of many marketing tools. The number of religious organizations interested in engaging in marketing practices has spawned a new category of consultants—church marketing. A search of the World Wide Web in May 2005 revealed several companies specializing in this field including:

<www.churchmarketing.com>
<www.outreach.com>
<www.church-marketing.com>
<www.MustardSeedStudio.com>
<www.breakthroughChurch.com>
<www.churchmarketingsucks.com>

Marketing literature, therefore, has generally been unrestrained in its enthusiastic pursuit of broadening marketing thought into the religious realm.

Religious Literature

Attitudes toward marketing in the religious literature have been more mixed (cf. Cutler and Winans, 1999). Although some marketing theorists have published positive-oriented articles in the religious literature (e.g., Engel and Horton, 1975; Engel, 1977, 1991; McDaniel, 1989; Wrenn and Kotler, 1993; Wrenn, 1994), when attention is paid to marketing by theologians and other religious scholars, it is ambivalent at best or condemnatory at worst (see Tables 10 and 11).

An interesting phenomenon is evident in Table 9: the promarketing books were written by marketers in the late 1980s and early 1990s, followed by a "backlash" of antimarketing books written by religious authors in the mid-to-late 1990s. This antimarketing sentiment is unique to the broadening of marketing to include religious organizations—in no other not-for-profit arena can we find a series of entire books devoted to discussion of why marketing practices should not be adopted by organizational administrators. Although many leaders of religious organizations who continue to believe in the Wesleyan "whatever works" school of thought, and adopt marketing when it helps them achieve their goals, the antimarketing group

TABLE 9. Significant Books/Monographs Addressing Marketing and Religious Institutions

Author	Stance	Author(s) Background	Example Quotes
Barna (1988)	Promarketing; Defense; "How-to"	Business	"... I believe that developing a marketing orientation is precisely what the Church needs to do if we are to make a difference in the spiritual health of this nation" p. 12
Day (1990)	Promarketing; Defense	Pastor; Business	"... [this] book is aimed at encouraging a more enlightened attitude toward the marketing process in the context of Christian ministry" p. 8
Pearson and Hisrich (1990)	Promarketing; "How-to"; Fictionalized	Religious administration; Academic	"But you're saying," said Brooks, "that the church should do a market survey first" p. 44
Barna (1992)	Promarketing; Defense; "How-to"	Business	"... the reality is that every church is engaged in marketing" p. 22
Shawchuck et al. (1992)	Promarketing; Defense; "How-to"	Pastor; Academic; Business	"Marketing is not an end for the religious organization; rather, it is a tool—a means to more effectively carry out the mission and ministry of the religious organization" p. 21
Shelley and Shelley (1992)	Accommodation between marketing and religious tradition	Pastors	"... the best way to approach ... ministry today is to acknowledge its ambidextrous calling... Ministry must be both faithful and effective" p. 17
Stevens and Loudon (1992)	Promarketing; "How-to"	Academic; Business	"Church/ministry marketing is the analysis, planning, and management of voluntary exchanges between a church or ministry and its constituents for the purpose of satisfying the needs of both parties" p. 3
Webster (1992)	Antimarketing	Pastor	"A church could master the art of marketing but neglect faithfulness, justice, and mercy. The 'successful' church may be more entertaining than edifying and more exalting than holy" p. 56
Guinness (1993)	Antimarketing	Writer	"Our present concern is [with] the range of problems that grow from the [church growth] movements' uncritical use of such insights and tools of modernity as management and marketing" p. 25

155

TABLE 9 *(continued)*

Author	Stance	Authors Background	Example Quotes
MacArthur (1993)	Antimarketing	Pastor	"Unfortunately, the market-driven ministry philosophy appeals to the very worst mood of our age. It caters to people whose first love is themselves and who care not for God . . ." p. 28
Moore (1994)	History of American religion and the marketplace	Historian; Academic	"A major thesis of this book . . . has to do not with the disappearance of religion, but its commodification, the ways in which churches have grown by participation in the market" p. 5
Wells (1994)	Antimarketing	Theologian	"I want to take a close look at the growing enterprise of marketing Christian faith—an enterprise that promises so much success but comes packaged with values that are quite destructive to Christian faith" p. 59
Considine (1995c)	Promarketing; "How-to"	Academic	". . . the challenges and problems confronting churches today necessitate . . . consideration of how a marketing orientation may enable them to . . . grow and prosper" p. 3
Kenneson and Street (1997)	Antimarketing	Theologian	". . . Our dispute with church marketers is most accurately characterized as a fundamental disagreement about the very identity, character, and mission of the church itself" p. 17
Gibbs (2000)	Primarily antimarketing	Theologian	". . . all marketing insights must be viewed with caution and discernment. They can be used for wrong ends and can be misused in a manipulative manner" p. 47

TABLE 10. Conceptual Articles in the Religion Literature

Author/Date	Purpose	Key Words	Stance	Use/Source	Comments
Calian, 1983	Investigate use of marketing by pastors	Selling, Marketing, Mission	Promarketing	Theoretical	Professor of theology makes a case for need to use "selling" approaches by pastors in their work
Gleason, 1984	Examine use of marketing of pastoral care to health care settings	Pastoral care, Pastoral counseling, Chaplaincy	Promarketing	Application	Reacts to the cutbacks in health care chaplaincy with some marketing ideas
Lageman, 1984	Explore application of marketing principles to pastoral counseling	Pastoral counseling, Marketing	Promarketing	Application	Identifies and illustrates application of marketing principles as they relate to pastoral counseling
Parro, 1991	Discuss pros and cons of using marketing by churches	Promarketing, Antimarketing	Neutral	Theoretical	Describes several positive contributions of marketing orientation to the church; Several areas where marketing orientation is at odds with biblical views
Kenneson, 1993	Discuss marketing for churches from theological perspective	Theology, Marketing orientation, Needs	Antimarketing	Theoretical	Explains why it is inappropriate for churches to do marketing; Provides presuppositions and argues them
Wrenn, 1994	Examines objections to use of marketing by religious organizations	Church marketing	Promarketing	Theoretical	Lists specific objections that have been leveled at use of marketing by religious organizations; Provides response to critics which supports use of marketing
Wells, 1995	Critique of use of marketing by churches	Church marketing	Antimarketing	Theoretical	Condemns use of marketing by religious organizations; Marketing is a cultural tool of church growth movement; Impossible to market faith
Ogletree, 1995-1996	Discusses propositions relating use of marketing to religious organizations	Market orientation, Critique	Neutral	Theoretical	Yale Divinity School dean discusses pros and cons of applying marketing to religious organizations; Marketing contributes to goals; Use with caution to remain focused on the Divine
Belokonny, 1997	Examine and respond to criticisms of church marketing	Biblical, Theological, Church marketing	Promarketing	Theoretical	Provides theological support for application of marketing to religious organizations

TABLE 11. Empirical Articles in the Religion Literature

Author/Date	Purpose	Key Words	Sample	Findings
Netteburg et al., 1987	Describe use of geodemography by churches	Geodemography	265,761 Donnelly Database households	Identifies which geodemographic segments Seventh-Day Adventist Church members belong
Dudley et al., 1989	Gedemographic profiling of denominational members	Geodemography	265,761 Donnelly Database households	Further profiling from 1987 article
McDaniel, 1989	Determine clergy's views of marketing	Clergy, Survey, Marketing	290 pastors; 261 general public	Clergy have generally positive attitude toward use of marketing; Marketing directed to church members was viewed by both pastors and public as most appropriate

is philosophically opposed to the use of marketing. This opposition centers around their perception of the nature of marketing and the marketer's worldview, and their belief that these are fundamentally at odds with the nature of religion and religious institutions. Thus, it could be said that the proponents and opponents of marketing among religious leaders both feel as they do about marketing for the same reason—it "works."

CONCLUSION

The religious marketing literature continues to grow at a healthy rate. Unlike controversies that arose when marketing was applied to other not-for-profit areas, however, the controversy surrounding the use of marketing by religious organizations will not be resolved by a demonstration that marketing can generate desired results. Theologians who stand in opposition to marketing have previously gone on record as being philosophically opposed to much of what the "church growth" proponents, who are generally favorably inclined toward marketing, seek to achieve. Moreover, this opposition is not based upon an incorrect understanding of the nature of marketing. A careful reading of many of the articles and books opposing the adoption of marketing reveals an accurate perception of marketing thought. Rather, it is a profound belief on the part of marketing critics that such thinking is contrary to the philosophies inherent in the mission and nature of religious organizations. Future attention could profitably be given to an exploration, from a marketer's perspective, of those philosophical differences, as well as a continuation of sowing the marketing seed on fertile religious soil.

REFERENCES

Arndt, Johan (1978), "How Broad Should the Marketing Concept Be?" *Journal of Marketing,* 42 (January), 101-103.

Ashley, W. B. (1917), *Church Advertising: Its Why and How,* Philadelphia, PA: J. B. Lippincott Company.

Attaway, Jill S., James Boles, and Rodger B. Singley (1996), "Understanding Consumers' Determinant Attributes in Church Selection," *Journal of Ministry Marketing & Management,* 2 (1), 15-20.

Barna, George (1988), *Marketing the Church,* Colorado Springs, CO: NavPress.

———— (1992), *A Step-by-Step Guide to Church Marketing,* Ventura, CA: Regal Books.

Bartels, Robert (1976), *The History of Marketing Thought,* Second Edition, Columbus, OH: Grid, Inc.

Belokonny, Mark J. (1997), "Biblical and Theological Issues of Church Marketing," *Journal of American Society for Church Growth,* (Spring), 35-61.

Berry, Leonard L. (1980), "Services Marketing Is Different," *Business,* (May-June), 24-29.

Busenitz, Lowell, Stephen W. McDaniel, and Chung-Ming Lau (1990), "Focused versus General Marketing Strategies in a Religious Setting," *Journal of Professional Services Marketing,* 6 (1), 167-181.

Calian, Carnegie Samuel (1983), "Marketing the Church's Ministry," *The Christian Ministry,* 14 (3), 22-23.

Carman, James M. (1987), "Rules for Church Promotion Decisions," *Decision Sciences,* 18 (Fall), 598-616.

Case, Francis H. (1921), *Handbook of Church Advertising,* New York: The Abingdon Press.

Clinton, Roy J., Stan Williamson, and Robert E. Stevens (1996), "Constituent Surveys As an Input in the Strategic Planning Process for Churches and Ministries: Part II," *Journal of Ministry Marketing & Management,* 2 (1), 47-59.

Considine, John J. (1995a), "Broadening the Marketing Concept to Churches," *Journal of Ministry Marketing & Management,* 1 (1), 25-34.

———— (1995b), "Developing a Marketing Research Process for Religious Organizations, *Journal of Ministry Marketing & Management,* 1 (2), 29-41.

———— (1995c), *Marketing Your Church,* Kansas City, MO: Sheed and Ward.

———— (1996a), "Attracting Baby Boomers Back to the Church," *Journal of Ministry Marketing & Management,* 2 (1), 33-45.

———— (1996b), "A Market Segmentation Approach for Religious Organizations," *Journal of Ministry Marketing & Management,* 2 (1), 1-13.

———— (1999), "Developing Appropriate Promotional Strategies for Religious Organizations," *Journal of Ministry Marketing & Management,* 5 (1), 23-36.

Considine, John J. and Greg Lepak (1998), "Utilizing Conjoint Analysis in Church Preference Studies: An Exploratory Study, *Journal of Ministry Marketing & Management,* 4 (1), 57-65.

Culliton, James W. (1959), "A Marketing Analysis of Religion," *Business Horizons,* 2 (Spring), 85-92.

Cutler, Bob D. (1991), "Religion and Marketing: Important Research Area or a Footnote in the Literature?," *Journal of Professional Services Marketing,* 8 (1), 153-164.

Cutler, Bob D. and William A. Winans (1999), "What Do Religion Scholars Say About Marketing? Perspectives from the Religion Literature," *Journal of Professional Services Marketing,* 18 (2), 133-145.

Day, Dan (1990), *A Guide to Marketing Adventism,* Boise, ID: Pacific Press Publishing Association.

Dudley, Roger L., Bruce Wrenn, and Slimen Saliba (1989), "Who Are(n't) We Baptizing?" *Ministry,* (April), 4-8.

Dunlap, B. J., Patricia Gaynor, and W. Daniel Rountree (1983), "The Viability of Marketing in a Religious Setting: An Empirical Analysis," *Proceedings,* Southern Marketing Association, Carbondale, IL: The Southern Marketing Association and Southern Illinois University, 45-48.

Dunlap, B. J. and W. Daniel Rountree (1982), "The Role of Marketing in a Religious Setting: Concepts and Applications," *Proceedings,* Southern Marketing Association, Carbondale, IL: The Southern Marketing Association and Southern Illinois University, 48-51.

Elliot, Ernest Eugene (1917) *How to Fill the Pews,* Cincinnati: Standard Pub. Co.

——— (1920), *How to Advertise a Church,* New York: George H. Doran Company.

Ellis, William T. (1913), *Advertising the Church.*

Engel, James F. (1977), *How Can I Get Them to Listen?,* Grand Rapids, MI: Zondervan.

Engel, James R. (1991), "Using Research Strategically in Urban Ministry," *Urban Mission,* (March), 6-12.

Engel, James R. and H. Wilbert Horton (1975), *What's Gone Wrong With the Harvest?: A Communication Strategy for the Church and World Evangelization,* Grand Rapids, MI: Zondervan.

Ensley, Frances Gerald (1958), *John Wesley: Evangelist,* Nashville, TN: Tidings.

Gazda, Gregory, Carolyn I. Anderson, and Donald Sciglimpaglia (1983), "Marketing and Religion: An Assessment of the Clergy," *Proceedings,* Southern Marketing Association, Carbondale, IL: The Southern Marketing Association and Southern Illinois University, 78-80.

Gibbs, Eddie (2000), *ChurchNext,* Downers Grove, IL: InterVarsity Press.

Ginter, James L. and W. Wayne Talarzyk (1978), "Applying the Marketing Concept to Design New Products," *Journal of Business Research,* 6 (January), 51-66.

Gleason, John J. Jr. (1984), "The Marketing of Pastoral Care and Counseling, Chaplaincy, and Clinical Pastoral Education," *The Journal of Pastoral Care,* 38 (4), 264-267.

Guinness, O. (1993), *Dining with the Devil,* Grand Rapids, MI: Baker Book House.

Hamilton, Jay Benson (1879), *Empty Churches, and How to Fill Them,* New York: Phillips & Hunt.

Hines, Randall W. (1996a), "Church Advertising Practices and Perceptions," *Journal of Ministry Marketing & Management,* 2 (1), 81-95.

―――― (1996b), "Church News Releases: Spreading the Word Economically," *Journal of Ministry Marketing & Management,* 2 (2), 47-55.

Hirschman, Elizabeth C. (1983), "Aesthetics, Ideologies, and the Limits of the Marketing Concept," *Journal of Marketing,* 47 (Summer), 45-55.

Horne, Suzanne and Alison Logie (2000), "Pupils' Attitudes to Religious and Moral Education: Is There a Need for Marketing?" *Journal of Ministry Marketing & Management,* 5 (2), 67-82.

Horne, Suzanne and Andrew McAuley (1999), "Church Services: A Conceptual Case for Marketing," *Journal of Ministry Marketing & Management,* 4 (2), 23-35.

Houston, Franklin S. (1986), "The Marketing Concept: What it Is and What it Is Not," *Journal of Marketing,* (April), 81-87.

Hull, Brooks B. and Frederick Bold (1989), "Toward an Economic Theory of the Church," *International Journal of Social Economics,* (July), 5-15.

Hunt, Shelby (1983), *Marketing Theory,* Homewood, IL: Irwin.

Iannoccone, Laurence R. (1992), "Religious Markets and the Economics of Religion," *Social Compass,* (March), 121-131.

Jones, Harold B. Jr. (1999), "Successful Pastoral Leadership Behaviors," *Journal of Ministry Marketing & Management,* 4 (2), 75-84.

Joseph, W. Benoy and Marion S. Webb (2000), "Marketing Your Church with Advertising and Promotion Strategies That Work," *Journal of Ministry Marketing & Management,* 6 (1), 19-33.

Kenneson, Philip D. (1993), "Selling [Out] The Church in the Marketplace of Desire," *Modern Theology,* 9 (October), 326-349.

Kenneson, Philip D. and James L. Street (1997), *Selling Out the Church,* Nashville, TN: Abingdon Press.

Kilbourne, Brock and James T. Richardson (1988), "Paradigm Conflict, Types of Conversion, and Conversion Theories," *Sociological Analysis,* 50 (1), 1-21.

Kotler, Philip and Sidney J. Levy (1969), "Broadening the Concept of Marketing," *Journal of Marketing,* 33 (1), 10-15.

Lageman, August G. (1984), "Marketing Pastoral Counseling," *The Journal of Pastoral Care,* 38 (4), 274-276.

Lee, Richard R. (1992), "Religious Practice As Social Exchange: An Explanation of the Empirical Findings," *Sociological Analysis,* 53 (17), 1-35.

LeMasters, Karen L. (1988), "Non Profit Marketing for Religious Institutions: Our New Frontier," *Journal of Marketing Management,* 3 (1), 208-220.

Luck, David J. (1969), "Broadening the Concept of Marketing—Too Far," *Journal of Marketing,* (1), 53-55.

MacArthur, John F. Jr. (1993), *Ashamed of the Gospel,* Wheaton, IL: Crossway Books.

McDaniel, Stephen (1986), "Church Advertising: Views of the Clergy and General Public," *Journal of Advertising,* 15 (1), 24-29.

——— (1989), "The Use of Marketing Techniques by Churches: A National Survey," *Review of Religious Research,* 31 (December), 175.

Mehta, Sanjay S. and Gurinderjit B. Mehta (1995), "Marketing of Churches: An Empirical Study of Important Attributes," *Journal of Professional Services Marketing,* 13 (1), 53.

Moncreif, William C., Charles W. Lamb Jr., and Sandra Hile Hart (1986), "Marketing the Church," *Journal of Professional Services Marketing,* 1 (Summer), 55-60.

Montgomery, Robert D., Mark A. Mitchell, Daniel L. Bauer, and Gregory B. Turner (2000), "A Changing Marketplace: Marketing Religion and Spirituality to Generation X," *Journal of Ministry Marketing & Management,* 6 (1), 35-51.

Moore, R. Laurence (1994), *Selling God,* New York, NY: Oxford University Press.

Muncy, James A. (1996), "Market Differentiation Strategies for Church Growth," *Journal of Ministry Marketing & Management,* 2 (2), 1-13.

Murray, Vernon Q. (1997), "In-House and External Secondary Data Sources for a Ministry Donor Information System," *Journal of Ministry Marketing & Management,* 3 (1), 71-85.

Netteburg, Kermit, Bruce Wrenn, Slimen Saliba, and Roger Dudley (1987), "Marketing Our Church," *Ministry,* (February), 4-8.

Nickels, William G. (1974), "Conceptual Conflicts in Marketing," *Journal of Economics and Business,* (Winter), 140-143.

Ogletree, Thomas W. (1995-1996), "Telling Our Story: Can Marketing Help Us?" *Quarterly Review,* 337.

Parker, R. Stephen and John L. Kent (1999), "The Use of Research in the Formulation of Church Marketing Strategies," *Journal of Ministry Marketing & Management,* 5 (1), 37-49.

Parro, Craig (1991), "Church Growth's Two Faces," *Christianity Today,* 35 (7), 19.

Pearson, John W. and Robert D. Hisrich (1990), *Marketing Your Ministry,* Brentwood, TN: Wolegmuth and Hyatt.

Primeaux, Patrick, Larry W. Boone, and Mary Maury (1997), "What Do Catholics Want? Ascertaining Parishioner Satisfaction," *Journal of Ministry Marketing & Management,* 3 (2), 29-51.

Reisner, Christian Fichthorne (1913), *Church Publicity: The Modern Way to Compel Them to Come In,* New York: The Methodist Book Concern.

Saunders, Paula (2000), "Increasing Church Member Satisfaction and Retention," *Journal of Ministry Marketing & Management,* 5 (2), 51-66.

Shawchuck, Norman, Philip Kotler, Bruce Wrenn, and Gustave Rath (1992), *Marketing for Congregations,* Nashville, TN: Abingdon Press.

Shelly, Bruce and Marshall Shelley (1992), *Consumer Church,* Downers Grove, IL: Inter Varsity Press.

Sherman, Ann and James F. Devlin (1998), "Church of England Clergy Attitudes Toward Marketing Activities: A Qualitative Perspective," *Journal of Ministry Marketing & Management,* 4 (1), 67-77.

Smith, Herbert Heebner (1922), *Church and Sunday School Publicity,* Philadelphia, PA: The Westminster Press.

Stark, Rodney and William Sims Bainbridge (1987), *A Theory of Religion,* New York, NY: Lang.

Stelzle, Charles (1908), *Principles of Successfull Church Advertising,* New York: Fleming H. Revell Company.

Stevens, Robert E., O. Jeff Harris, and J. Gregory Chachere (1996), "Increasing Member Commitment in a Church Environment," *Journal of Ministry Marketing & Management,* 2 (2), 69-95.

Stevens, Robert E. and David L. Loudon (1992), *Marketing for Churches and Ministries,* Binghamton, NY: The Haworth Press.

Stevens, Robert E., David L. Loudon, and R. Wade Paschal (1995), "Clergy Evaluations of the Appropriateness of Marketing Activities: A Re-Examination," *Journal of Ministry Marketing & Management,* 1 (1), 85-96.

Stout, Harry S. (1991), *The Divine Dramatist,* Grand Rapids, MI: William B. Erdmann Publishing Co.

Webb, Marion, S. W. Benoy Joseph, Kurt Schimmel, and Christopher Moberg (1998), "Church Marketing: Strategies for Retaining and Attracting Members," *Journal of Professional Services Marketing,* 17 (2), 1-16.

Webster, Douglas D. (1992), *Selling Jesus,* Downers Grove, IL: Inter Varsity Press.

Wells, David F. (1994), *God In the Wasteland,* Grand Rapids, MI: William B. Ermann Publishing Company.

——— (1995), "Marketing the Church: Analysis and Assessment, Part I," *Faith & Ministry,* 12 (Spring), 3-20.

White, Darin W. (1998), "Determinants of Altruistic Volunteering: An Empirical Assessment," *Journal of Ministry Marketing & Management,* 4 (1), 33-55.

Wrenn, Bruce (1992), "Product Mix Development for Religious Organizations," *Proceedings,* Atlantic Marketing Association, ed. Donald L. Thompson, The Atlantic Marketing Association, the University of Central Florida, and Georgia Southern University, 8 (October), 424-427.

——— (1993a), "The Role of Marketing for Religious Organizations," *Journal of Professional Services Marketing,* 8 (2), 237.

——— (1993b), "What Business Can Teach Religious Organizations About Customer Service," *Journal of Professional Services Marketing,* 8 (2), 251.

——— (1994), "Can (Should) Religion Be Marketed?" *Quarterly Review,* (Summer), 117-134.

——— (1995), "Internal Marketing: How a Market Orientation Can Be Used to Deliver Satisfaction to Current Members," *Journal of Ministry Marketing & Management,* 1 (2), 3-28.

——— (1997), "The Market Orientation Construct: Measurement and Scaling Issues," *Journal of Marketing Theory and Practice,* (Summer), 31-54.

Wrenn, Bruce and Philip Kotler (1993), "The Marketing of Parochial Schooling Modeled as an Exchange Process," *Journal of Research on Christian Education,* (Spring), 119-134.

Wrenn, Bruce and Slimen Saliba (1988), "New Approaches to Segmenting and Targeting for Religious Institutions," *Journal of Midwest Marketing,* (Spring), 229-235.

——— (1993), "Marketing Marketing to Religious 'Marketers,' " *Proceedings,* Atlantic Marketing Association, ed. Donald L. Thompson, The Atlantic Marketing Association, the University of Central Florida, and Georgia Southern University, 9 (October), 396-399.

——— (1995), "Religious Marketing is Different," *Proceedings,* Midwest Marketing Association, eds. E. Wayne Chandler and Michael d'Amico, The Midwest Marketing Association and Eastern Illinois University, 1-7.

Wrenn, Bruce, Norman Shawchuck, Philip Kotler, and Gustave Rath (1995), "What Does It Mean for Pastors to Adopt a Market Orientation?" *Journal of Ministry Marketing & Management,* 1 (1), 5-23.

Wymer, Walter W. Jr. (1997), "Church Volunteers: Classification, Recruitment, and Retention," *Journal of Ministry Marketing & Management,* 3 (2), 61-70.

——— (1998), "Strategic Marketing of Church Volunteers," *Journal of Ministry Marketing & Management,* 4 (1), 1-11.

——— (1999a), "Becoming Marketing Oriented: Applying the Marketing Concept in Small Group Ministry Settings," *Journal of Ministry Marketing & Management,* 4 (2), 37-46.

——— (1999b), "A Qualitative Analysis of Church Volunteerism: Motives for Service, Motives for Retention, and Perceived Benefits/Rewards from Volunteering," *Journal of Ministry Marketing & Management,* 5 (1), 51-64.

——— (2000), "Making Loyal Customers: Helping Our Youth to Be Loyal to Christ, Church, and Family Values," *Journal of Ministry Marketing & Management,* 6 (1), 1-10.

Zaleski, Peter A. and Charles E. Zech (1995), "The Effectiveness of Various Solicitation Methods in Raising Member Contributions: Evidence from the Presbyterian Church ('As Ye Sow, So Shall Ye Reap')," *Journal of Ministry Marketing & Management,* 1 (1), 97-104.

Appendix B

Writers/Researchers
in Church and Religious
Organization Marketing

The following list serves as a general guide to those who are writing and/or doing research in church and religious marketing. It is not intended to be a complete list of all writers/researchers.

Andrews, Brett K.	LeTourneau University, TX
Arndt, Johan	Graduate School of Business, Columbia University, New York City, NY
Attaway, Jill S.	Illinois State University, Normal, IL
Auken, Philip Van	Baylor University, Waco, TX
Baack, Donald	Department of Management and Marketing, Pittsburg State University, KS
Baer, Timothy L.	Suffolk Community Church, Suffolk, VA; Founder, Baer Equipment Systems
Baeur, Daniel L.	Bellarmine College, Louisville, KY
Bainbridge, William Sins	Albany State University of New York Press, NY
Barna, George	Biola University; President, Barna Research Group, Glendale, CA
Bartels, Robert	Ohio State University
Boissoneau, Robert	RBI Consulting, Chandler, AZ
Boles, James	Georgia State University, Atlanta

Bond III, Edward U.	Foster College of Business Administration, Peoria, IL
Boone, Larry W.	Assistant Provost for University Planning
Brien, David	Screven Baptist Association, Summerville
Brown, Valerie K.	The Samuel D. Proctor School of Theology, Virginia Union University, Richmond; President, Valerie K. Brown, CPA, PC
Burns, Cynthia F.	College of Administration and Management, Regent University, Virginia Beach, VA
Burnside, Burnie R.	First Church of the Nazarene, Denton, TX; President, New Life Evangelical Ministries, Inc.
Byren Van III, Harry J.	Division of Business and Management, Roberts Wesleyan College, Rochester, NY
Cardente, Reverend Edward S.	St. Anthony Parish, North Providence, RI
Carman, James M.	University of California, Berkeley
Casey, Michael K.	Hendersen State University, Arkadelphia, AK
Cecil, Wayne H.	University of Southern Mississippi, Long Beach
Chachere, Gregory J.	Appaloosa, LA
Cheatham, Carole	Monroe, LA
Cheatham, Leo	Monroe, LA
Chester, Michael C.	Norfolk State University, VA
Chonko, Lawrence B. Holloway	Baylor University, Waco, TX
Clinton, Roy J.	Department of Management and Marketing, University of Louisiana, Monroe
Clow, Kenneth	University of Louisiana, Monroe

Cole, Henry S.	College of Business Administration, University of Louisiana, Monroe
Considine, John	Department of Business Administration, Le Moyne College, Syracuse, NY
Cotter, Michael J.	Seidman School of Business, Grand Valley State University, Allendale, MI
Davis, Dale	Colgate Rochester Divinity School, Rochester, NY
Devlin, James F.	Nottingham, UK
Duncan, John B.	University of Louisiana, Monroe
Dunn, Paul	University of Louisiana, Monroe
Duvall, Cheryl King	Stetson School of Business, Atlanta, GA
Dyson, David A.	Oral Roberts University, Tulsa, OK
Engel, James F.	Eastern College, PA
Fagan, Ralph	Oral Roberts University, Tulsa, OK
Felton Jr., Edward L.	Samford University, Birmingham, AL
Fram, Eugene H.	Institute of Technology, Rochester, NY
Hamon, Tim T.	Christian International Ministries Network, Santa Rosa Beach, FL
Harper, Betty S.	Middle Tennessee State University
Harper, Phil	Middle Tennessee State University
Harris, Jeff O.	University of Louisiana, Monroe
Hartman, Sandra	University of New Orleans,
Henley Jr., James A.	The University of Tennessee at Chattanooga
Herrington, Duncan J.	Radford University, VA
Hines, Randall W.	Department of Communication, East Tennessee State University, Johnson City
Hirschman, Elizabeth C.	Princeton, NJ

Hisrich, Robert D.	The Weather Head School of Management, Case Western Reserve University, Cleveland, OH
Hix, John L.	Louisiana College, Pineville
Horne, Suzanne	University of Stirling, Scotland, UK
Horvath, Jeffrey S.	Tulsa, OK
Hoskins, Margaret	School of Business, Henderson State University, Arkadelphia, AR
Hunt, Carle	Regent University, Virginia Beach, VA
Hunt, JoAnna	Tidewater Community College, Virginia Beach, VA
Irwin, Craig E.	Albion Alliance Church, NY
Jones Jr., Harold B.	Mercer University, Macon, GA
Jordan, Robert E.	University of Wisconsin–Superior
Joseph, Benoy W.	Cleveland State University, OH
Kent, John L.	Southwest Missouri State University, Springfield
Kotler, Philip	Northwestern University, Evanston, IL
Knipp, Ken	Great Lakes Region, Young life
Lantos, Geoffrey P.	Stonehill College, North Easton, MA
Laverdiere, Raymond G.	Norfolk State University, VA
Lawrence, Lesa W.	University of Louisiana, Monroe
Lenell, Martin Wayne	Diocese of Rockford, IL
Lepak, Greg	LeMoyne College, Syracuse, NY
Levy, Sidney J.	Northwestern University, Chicago, IL
Logie, Alison	University of Stirling, Scotland, UK
Loudon, David L.	University of Louisiana, Monroe
Luck, David J.	Southern Illinois University
Maes, Jeanne D.	University of South Alabama, Mobile
Mansfield, Phylis	Penn State University, PA
Martin, Rinne T.	Oral Roberts University, Tulsa, OK

Maury, Mary	St. John's University, Queens, NY
McAuley, Andrew	University of Stirling, Scotland, UK
McConkey, William C.	University of Louisiana, Monroe
McDaniel, Stephen W.	Graduate School of Business, Texas A&M University, College Station
Migliore, Henry R.	Northeastern State University, Tulsa, OK
Miller, Robert J.	Philadelphia, PA
Mitchell, Mark A.	University of South Carolina, Spartanburg
Montgomery, Robert D.	University of Evansville, IN
Moore, Laurence R.	Cornell University, Ithaca, NY
Muncy, James A.	Valdosta State University, GA
Murray, Vernon Quinton	Marist College, Poughkeepsie, NY
Nathan, Maria L.	University of Texas, San Antonio
Nickels, William G.	University of Maryland, College Park
Notarantanio, Elaine M.	Bryant College, Smithfield, RI
Orwig, Linda	Worthy Life Ministries, Macon, GA
Orwig, Robert A.	Mercer University, Macon, GA
Parfet, Robert A.	Archdiocese of Philadelphia
Parker, Stephen R.	Southwest Missouri State University, Springfield
Paschal, Wade R. Jr.	First United Methodist Church, Tulsa, OK
Pinson, Kathleen B.	Mercer University, Macon, GA
Primeaux, Patrick S.M.	Department of Theology and Religious Studies, Saint John's University, Jamaica, NY
Quigley Jr., Charles J.	Bryant College, Smithfield, RI
Rath, Gustave	Northwestern University, Evanston, IL

Reed, Marlene M.	School of Business, Samford University, Birmingham, AL
Roller, Robert H.	LeTournaeu University, Longview, TX
Ruddick, Morris E.	The Ruddick Int'l Group, Aurora, CO
Rupp, William T.	Robert Morris College, Pittsburgh, PA
Saunders, Paula M.	Wright State University, Dayton, OH
Schewe, Charles	University of Massachusetts, Amherst
Sciglimpaglia, Donald	University of Colorado
Shawchuck, Norman	Shawchuck & Associates, Ltd., Elgin, ND
Sherman, Ann	UK
Singley, Rodger B.	Illinois State University, Normal
Smith, Alan D.	Robert Morris College
Smith, Deborah J.	Pepperdine University
Spreng, Richard A.	Michigan State University, East Lansing
Stark, Rodney	University of Washington, Seattle
Stevens, Robert E.	University of Louisiana, Monroe
Talarzyk, Wayne W.	Ohio State University, Columbus
Turner, Gregory B.	College of Charleston, SC
Unseth, Allan D.	Norfolk State University, Regent University, Virginia Beach, VA
Vokurka, Robert J.	Texas A&M University, College Station
Wakefield, Kirk L.	University of Mississippi, University, MS
Webb, Marion S.	Cleveland State University, OH
Wells, Richard C.	Tulane University; University of New Orleans
White, Darin W.	Union University, Jackson, TN

Williamson, Stan	University of Louisiana, Monroe
Winston, Bruce E.	Regent University, School of Business, Virginia Beach, VA
Woodworth, Stephen J.	Marketing Group, World Vision, Inc., Monrovia, CA
Wrenn, Bruce	Indiana University South Bend
Wymer Jr., Walter W.	Jacksonville University, FL
Zaleski, Peter A.	Villanova University, Philadelphia, PA
Zech, Charles	Villanova University, Philadelphia, PA

Index

Access, 1, 12, 80
Accessibility, 74
Active listening, 2, 3
Activity cost analysis, 32
Adoption process, 4, 5, 87
Advertising data, 108
Advertising message, 5, 6, 86, 87
Advertising strategy, 5
Affective message, 6
AIDA model, 4
AIO (activities, interests, opinions), 115
Analysis of selected cases, 56
Analytical tools, 39
Atmosphere, 6, 57, 58, 75, 119
Attendance control, 106
Attendance objective, 99, 106
Attitude measurement, 8, 9, 11

Baptist, 20, 166
Benefits of marketing, 11
Best location, 73, 97
Bottom-up approach, 109
Brand equity, 12, 13
Broadcast media, 96
Buber, Martin, 81
Budgets, 13

Catholic, 72
Cause-related marketing, 14
Christian, 19, 33, 34, 95, 159, 162, 163, 167
Church organization, 71, 104
Cognitive message, 6
Communication elements, 120
Communication methods, 17

Compensation, 109, 111
Competition, 18
Competitive advantage, 13, 20, 21, 22, 27, 68, 98, 140
Constituent analysis, 24, 83, 89
Constituent attitudes, 35, 84
Constituent behavior, 25, 101
Constituent objectives, 101
Constituent service, 26, 27
Constituent test, 95, 96
Constituent type, 106, 110
Contribution analysis, 29
Contribution objective, 100
Contribution sources, 32
Contribution/cost controls, 30
Controlling marketing activities, 34
Core benefits, 72
Core values, 70
Cost effective, 45
Costs to target audience, 36
Cross-sectional analysis, 44
Cross-sectional survey, 45
Customer service, 26, 42, 70, 93, 94

Data collection, 38, 40, 44, 117, 135
Data collection and analysis, 39, 84
Data mining, 41
Database marketing, 39, 40, 41, 42
Data-gathering instrument, 123. *See also* Questionnaire
Demographic characteristics, 45
Demographic data, 43
Demographics, 11, 43, 113, 116
Descriptive research, 43, 44, 55, 59, 128, 137
Design decisions, 57
Designing a questionnaire, 125

For Product Safety Concerns and Information please contact our
EU representative GPSR@taylorandfrancis.com Taylor & Francis
Verlag GmbH, Kaufingerstraße 24, 80331 München, Germany